CONTENTS

INTRODUCTION:
AFFLICTED WITH MADNESS

Every year, tens of millions of fans experience three heart-thumping, stomach-twisting, teeth-gnashing weeks in a national sports obsession officially known as the NCAA Division I Men's Basketball Tournament.

We all know it as March Madness. This annual ritual of triumphs and defeats, nail-biters and laughers, heroes and goats consumes our time like no other amateur sporting event. We study the brackets, analyze the teams, debate their chances and watch their games. We toss hundreds of millions of dollars into office pools and cost employers, according to one estimate, $237 million a day in lost productivity at work.

"With the exception of the National Football League,

there is no other sport with the fanatical following of the NCAAs, when you consider the office pools and parties in houses, dorms and bars," says CBS analyst Billy Packer, whose network shows the annual 63-game event under an 11-year contract worth a whopping $6 billion.

Why this fascination? It's the hoops version of reality television. The tournament creates new stars and hundreds of engrossing stories for us fans who since 1991 have been able to see every game live on television and, now, even on webcasts too.

We get to root for young men who haven't been tainted by multi-million-dollar contracts and endorsements playing their hearts out in do-or-die games. There are no second chances, no consolations. Lose, and it's over. And for many players, it's not just for the season but for their collegiate careers. So, however hard they played during the regular season, they play even harder now.

What makes this tournament so special is that every team has a chance, at least in the early rounds. That's the insanity behind March Madness. It isn't just about Duke and Kentucky and North Carolina. No, it's also about George Mason and Richmond and Hampton—the little guys, the Cinderellas, the Davids that beat Goliaths and the odds.

We are captivated because impressive win-loss records

don't guarantee success. Since 1976, when undefeated Indiana won the championship, 20 teams have entered the tournament unbeaten or with one setback through 2006. Guess how many have won the national title: none, zero, nada. Only six teams in this group—Indiana State, 1979; University of Nevada, Las Vegas, 1987 and 1991; Massachusetts, 1996; Duke, 1999; and Illinois 2005— even reached the Final Four. For those teams that won titles, the road to victory was pockmarked with peril. Forty champions won at least one playoff game by four points or less and 19 won at least one of those games by a single point.

We get a kick out of seeing unsung players emerge as clutch players and become stars. Who was that freshman for North Carolina who hit the game-winning basket against Georgetown in the 1982 championship game? Oh, yeah, a kid named Michael Jordan.

We are afflicted with madness because we yearn to see history in the making. Will any player ever score more points than the record 56 Bill Bradley tallied in 1965? Will any low seed ever win the title like No. 8 seed Villanova did in 1985? Will any game ever top Duke's 104–103 overtime heart-stopper over Kentucky in 1992?

As we anticipate the thrills and excitement of another round of March Madness, it's fun to look back at tournaments past, which is what this book is all about. It features interesting, funny, and poignant stories—on and off the basketball court—about the annual spectacle from its start in 1939 through 2006. It relives great moments and not-so-great moments and spotlights some of the most courageous, talented and gritty players—as well as some of the zaniest—ever to compete in the tourney.

Hopefully this book will get you revved up for the next NCAA Tournament. But then, you already are, aren't you?

THE
EARLY DAYS

Training for Victory

Train travel played a major role in the Oregon Ducks'
championship in the National Collegiate Athletic
Association's inaugural national basketball tournament in
1939.

When the NCAA announced at the beginning of the
season there would be a new tourney, Oregon coach
Howard Hobson figured if his team had a chance at the
title, it needed to toughen up and compete against schools
that played different styles. So over the Christmas break in
1938, he took his Ducks on a grueling three-week rail
journey to play top teams in the East and Midwest where,

compared to the West Coast, referees acted as if blowing their whistles was a sin. But the road trip was a success. Oregon won six of nine, strengthening the team's mettle and preparing it for a run at the championship.

At that time, only eight teams vied in the tournament—Texas, Oklahoma, Utah State, Villanova, Brown, Wake Forest, and the eventual final two, Oregon and the Ohio State Buckeyes.

The championship game was held at Patten Gym on the campus of Northwestern University in Evanston, Illinois. Before the contest, the crowd was treated to an exhibition game played under the rules and conditions at the time basketball was invented in 1891. Two 12-man teams of Northwestern intramural all-stars tried to sink a ball into a peach basket at both ends of the court. Members of the school's varsity basketball team stood with broomsticks under each basket to poke out the ball after each goal. Among the honored guests in the audience was Dr. James Naismith, the man who had invented basketball in Springfield, Massachusetts, 48 years earlier.

In the championship game, the Ducks jumped out to a quick lead that they never relinquished, by relying on an unrelenting fast break and a height advantage. Holding the Buckeyes' leading scorer, Jimmy Hull, to 12 points, Oregon coasted to a relatively easy 46–33 victory. Alluding to the Ducks's lengthy rail travels, the state's biggest paper, *The Oregonian*, ran the headline: "Wandering Webfoots Whip Ohio State."

The Ducks were simply in much better shape than the Buckeyes and ran them ragged. In his book, *Shooting Ducks: A History of University of Oregon Basketball*, Coach Hobson said that before the game he had a talk with team captain and guard Bobby Anet, who usually directed the fast break. "I told Bobby to make Ohio State call the first time-out and not to call any until we were really tired," recalled Hobson. "Ohio State called five time-outs, and we didn't call any.

"After the game, I said to Bobby, 'Why didn't you call a time-out and take a little rest when the game was pretty well in hand?' He said to me, 'You told me not to call a time-out unless we were tired, and, hell, we weren't tired.'"

Anet unintentionally caused a slight embarrassment at the presentation ceremony held at mid-court immediately after the game.

Throughout the contest, the shiny new trophy had been displayed on a courtside table. In the second half, Anet charged after a loose ball that was bouncing out of bounds. Unable to stop, he flew over the table, hit the trophy and knocked off the top piece, which was a figure of a basketball player. There was no time to fix it.

After the game, chagrined Big Ten Conference Commissioner John L. Griffith tried to hold onto the little figure when he presented the Ducks with the trophy, but it fell off. So he handed Anet the broken trophy without its top. The team returned home with the trophy in two pieces and had it repaired by a local jeweler. But the Ducks didn't mind. After all, they were the NCAA's first national champions.

As much as the train trip helped Oregon prepare for the title, the team was nearly derailed by a threatened riot on the long train ride home.

The town of The Dalles, Oregon, wanted to honor Ducks forward John Dick, its hometown hero, who led all scorers in the game with 15 points. The fine citizens of this small riverside community east of Portland took up a collection and purchased a gold watch and had it engraved. They wanted to present it to their star because tournament officials hadn't given out any individual awards or acknowledgments to the players.

Civic leaders contacted a railroad official and asked that the train from Chicago make an unscheduled stop at The Dalles so they could present their favorite son with a modest gift of appreciation. To their anger, the official refused the request. So they went over his head and appealed to his boss. He turned them down, too. They didn't give up. With the train due to pass through The Dalles in less than eight hours, shortly before dawn, the civic leaders managed to reach the president of the railroad late at night. They made their final pitch, which was less a plea and more of a demand: Either he ordered the train to stop at The Dalles for a brief ceremony or the townspeople would barricade the tracks.

The president found their argument persuasive and arranged for a ten-minute stop. At 5 a.m., the train pulled into the tiny station at The Dalles, where more than 2,000 early-risers cheered as the grateful city fathers presented Dick with the gold watch.

DID YOU KNOW . . .

- John Dick was the only leading scorer of an NCAA Tournament to become an admiral in the U.S. Navy. During his 32-year naval career, he commanded the aircraft carrier *Saratoga* for two years and served as chief of staff for all carrier forces in the Western Pacific.
- The 1939 championship was the only NCAA Tournament that John Naismith ever saw. The inventor of basketball died eight months later at the age of 78.
- The NCAA's first title is the only one that Oregon has ever won.

DID YOU KNOW . . . (CONTINUED)
- The Oregon Ducks's unofficial nickname was the Tall Firs. With a 6-foot-8 center and two 6-foot-4 forwards, the title-winning Ducks were considered extremely tall back then.

Frankly, My Dear, I Don't Give a Damn

The wife of Indiana coach Branch McCracken had a small hand in the team winning the 1940 championship—by defying him.

When McCracken brought his run-and-gun Hoosiers to Kansas City to face the Kansas Jayhawks in the title game, he told his men to stay in the hotel on game day until it was time to go to the arena. However, his wife Mary Jo, who was the team's mother hen, sensed that the players appeared awfully tense. After all, the Jayhawks were favored and playing in front of a friendly crowd at a venue that was practically in their backyard.

Mary Jo thought going to the movies would loosen the Hoosiers up. But there was a problem. She knew her husband didn't want his team attending movies on game days because he feared it would affect their eyesight.

Nevertheless, she sneaked the players out of the hotel

and to a movie theater to see the hit film of the year, *Gone with the Wind*. They returned to their rooms feeling less stressed about the upcoming game. Her scheme certainly seemed to work. Playing a spirited, fast-paced game, the Hurryin' Hoosiers (aka the Merry Macs) destroyed the Jayhawks, 60–42. And what if the worst had happened and Indiana lost? How angry would her husband have become? Mary Jo figured she had a unique insurance policy—her father was the president of Indiana University.

Amazingly, Indiana almost didn't go to the tournament even though it had been invited. The team needed the approval of a faculty athletics committee, which wasn't too keen on spending the money for the squad to participate. "It was a hard sale, this new tournament, taking up class time and all that," said Bob Hammel, longtime sports editor of the *Bloomington* (Indiana) *Herald-Times*. "William Breneman, a distinguished professor who was IU's faculty representative to the Big Ten at the time, told me years later about the contentious meeting when it was up to the committee to accept or reject the invitation. Young coach Branch McCracken was there, arguing his case. But Breneman said the intra-committee debate went hours into the night before grudging approval came for McCracken's team to go to this 'national' thing."

Besides being blessed with great talent, the Hoosiers

had another thing going for them—Tootsie, their four-legged good luck charm. A cross between a fox terrier and a spitz, Tootsie was owned by an avid IU fan, 71-year-old Charles P. McNabb. Seven times he had brought his dog to Indiana games, and seven times the Hoosiers had won. So when IU made it to the finals, McNabb brought Tootsie with him to Kansas City and into Municipal Auditorium, where the dog's perfect record remained intact.

"We didn't know what to expect because we had never seen Indiana. The only scouting report we had was a letter from a KU alumnus back there [in Indiana]."
—Kansas player Howard Engleman, after Indiana beat the Jayhawks for the 1940 title

DID YOU KNOW . . .

- In 1940, for the first time, the players in the championship game were given gifts by the NCAA. The presents were gold basketballs to wear on their key chains or pocket watches.
- Bob Allen is the only player in NCAA finals history to be the game's high scorer while playing on a team coached by his father. Allen, who scored 13 points, was the son of Kansas coach Phog Allen.

The Draft that Blew Away a Title Chance

College basketball players of today would love to be drafted. But that wasn't necessarily true during World War II, when being drafted had a whole different meaning. In fact, Illinois, which through 2006 had never won an NCAA basketball championship, lost its best chance for a title because of war.

The Whiz Kids, as they were nicknamed back then, had blown through the 1942–43 season by winning 17 of 18 games and averaging 58 points in an era when scores usually were in the low 40s. As Big Ten champions, they were the favorites to capture the NCAA crown.

But national security took precedence. Before the tournament began, three of the Illini's starters—Jack Smiley, Art Mathisen and Ken Menke—received their induction notices and had to report for duty immediately. That left only starters Gene Vance and Andy Phillip and reserves on the squad.

So when the team was officially invited to play in the tourney, Coach Doug Mills declined the bid. He had decided that if all five starters couldn't play, none would.

Three months after Wyoming defeated Georgetown, 46–34, for the national championship, Vance and his teammate Phillip answered their call to duty and served in battle in Europe.

Interviewed in 2005 by *Chicago Tribune* reporter David Haugh, Vance said Mills' decision was the right choice. However, he added, "I think not being able to go the NCAAs was the biggest disappointment I've ever had."

> **DID YOU KNOW . . .**
> • Illinois' Whiz Kids picked up their nickname after WGN radio broadcaster Jack Brickhouse said during one of their games, "Those kids really whiz by you."

One Team's Tragedy; Another Team's Triumph

The Utah Utes won the 1944 NCAA championship in part because of a tragic accident involving the Arkansas Razorbacks.

After finishing the regular season with an 18–3 record, the Utes were invited to both the NCAA Tournament and the National Invitation Tournament. The team chose the NIT because the payout was better, and it guaranteed that the players and coach could spend some fun time in New York City.

In the first round, Utah faced the 17–1 Kentucky Wildcats in Madison Square Garden. After battling to a

24–24 tie at halftime, Kentucky pulled away for a 46–38 victory. The only consolation for the disappointed Utah players was they would get to enjoy a day or two of sight-seeing.

But around 2 a.m. they were rousted out of their hotel beds and summoned to the room of their coach, Vadal Peterson. He told them that the NCAA had invited the Utes to play in its tournament as a last-minute replacement for Arkansas, which had bowed out because of a horrific automobile accident the day before near Fayetteville.

The station wagon that members of the Razorbacks were traveling in had a flat tire. Because there was no shoulder on the highway, the driver parked the vehicle on the road as far to the right as he could. As trainer Eugene Norris and starters Deno Nichols and Ben Jones were fixing the flat, another car plowed into them, killing Norris and severely injuring the two players. Nichols' right leg was broken and later amputated. Both of Jones' legs were broken and his back was fractured and he needed two years to recuperate.

Coach Peterson told his Utah players they could decline the invitation to play in the NCAA and instead explore New York, or they could catch an early-morning train for a two-day trip to Kansas City for the opening-round game against the Missouri Tigers. To a man, the Utes voted to play. They knew if they won their two games in Kansas City, they would return to New York to vie for the championship.

When they stepped foot on the court for the tip-off against Missouri, Utah made history as the first team to play in both the NIT and NCAA tourneys in the same year. The Utes downed the Tigers, 45–35, and then vanquished the heavily favored Iowa State Cyclones, 40–31.

The second victory was especially sweet for Utah because few people expected them to win—including tournament director Reaves Peters. Before the game, he had told Utah's team manager that the winner would need to catch the midnight train to New York. Peters had the audacity to say that since the Cyclones would probably win, he had checked the Iowa State players out of their hotel rooms and put their luggage in the Utes' rooms because he figured that since Utah would lose, they didn't need to leave until the next day.

Hours later it was Iowa State that had to spend the night in the hotel—its players had taken over Utah's rooms—while the Utes were swaying on the rails to New York City to take on the Dartmouth Indians (now known as the Big Green) for the championship.

As if Peters's affront weren't enough, the underdog Utes

faced even more disrespect the morning of the game. According to author Lee Benson, Utes assistant coach Pete Crouch overheard several Dartmouth players disparage Utah, considering the team so unworthy that they suggested playing an intra-squad scrimmage before the main contest so the fans could get their money's worth. In the locker room before the game, Crouch told the Utes what he had heard. That fired them up.

In the nip-and-tuck game, Utah led by two when Dartmouth's Frank McGuire nailed a basket with two seconds left that sent the game into overtime tied 36–36. With the score knotted 40–40 in the waning seconds of OT, Utah's Herb Wilkerson chased down an offensive rebound and tossed up an off-balance shot that went through the hoop at the buzzer. Utah—a team that was invited to the tourney only because of a horrendous accident—was the new NCAA champion.

DID YOU KNOW . . .

- Because their field house had been converted into an army barracks, the Utes had no home games and practiced in a church gym in Salt Lake City.

DID YOU KNOW . . . (CONTINUED)

- The Mountain States Conference (also known as the Skyline Conference) had suspended play for the duration of the war so Utah played mostly service and industrial teams.
- Utah had only nine players on its team—seven freshmen, one sophomore and one junior. Their average age was $18\frac{1}{2}$.
- One of Utah's starters was Wataru (Wat) Misaka, a Japanese-American whose nation was at war with the country of his ancestors. Because he lived outside the western military exclusion zone, he avoided being herded into one of the many detention camps that housed other Japanese-Americans. While playing throughout the war, he occasionally was the target of slurs from opposing teams and fans.
- The New York media referred to the Utes as the Blitz Kids after the underdogs surprised most everyone by winning the NCAA Tournament and then beating NIT champion St. John's of New York in a benefit game.

The Red Cross Games

For three years during World War II, the champion of the NCAA Tournament played the winner of the rival National Invitation Tournament in a benefit game.

The special contests, which were played at Madison Square Garden in New York, raised tens of thousands of dollars for the American Red Cross. But it also brought the NCAA tourney a new stature that it never lost.

Up until that time, the NIT was considered more prestigious—and with better teams—than the NCAA's event. But all that changed when the NCAA champs outclassed the NIT winners every time.

Two days after claiming the 1943 NCAA title, the Wyoming Cowboys played the NIT champion, St. John's Redmen (now known as the Red Storm). In front of 18,000 screaming fans, most of them pulling for the hometown Redmen, the two teams battled to a 46–46 tie at the end of regulation. Wyoming scored what would have been the game-winner in the final seconds, but the basket was waved off because the Cowboys had called for a time-out just before the shot was made. However, Wyoming prevailed in overtime, 52–47.

St. John's repeated as the NIT champ the next year and faced off against the Utah Utes at the Garden. A crowd of 18,125 raised $35,000 for the war effort and watched another exciting Red Cross game. Even though the Redmen were favored because they had beaten highly-regarded DePaul for the NIT title, they fell to the Blitz Kids, 43–36, behind the 17 points of Utah's freshman star,

Arnie Ferrin's.

In 1945, the last of the Red Cross benefit games was hyped by the New York media as the "Clash of the Titans" and the "Game of the Century." (Never mind that the century wasn't even half over yet.) That's because it brought together the game's two most dominant big men at the time—6-foot-10 George Mikan of the NIT champion DePaul Blue Demons and 7-foot Bob Kurland of the NCAA-winning Oklahoma A&M Aggies (now Oklahoma State Cowboys). Both players would become Basketball Hall of Famers.

Although Kurland was considered more agile and quicker than Mikan, the DePaul center was stronger and a better shooter. The showdown was a letdown for the fans.

Mikan fouled out after scoring nine points in 14 minutes. Kurland finished with 14 points as the Aggies rallied from a 26–21 halftime deficit to win 52–44.

With its champions the winners of all three Red Cross games against the NIT's best, the NCAA Tournament proved it was now the premier event in college basketball.

The Orphans Of Worcester

The basketball team from the College of the Holy Cross had a lot going against it during the 1946–47 season. The Jesuit school was small, with an enrollment of only 1,400 young men. The basketball program was always short of money and had little to spend on recruiting. The team had no gymnasium on its Worcester, Massachusetts, campus, so the players practiced in an old converted barn. And what they called "home games" really weren't, because their home court was 40 miles away in Boston. Oh, and the team had no seniors, just two juniors, and only one player taller than 6-foot-3.

Yet, these hoop orphans defied logic and won the 1947 NCAA championship.

Although all the Crusaders were underclassmen, many were veterans in every sense of the word. Six of the ten players had served in the military during World War II.

Under the disciplined approach of their coach, Alvin "Doggie" Julian, Holy Cross charged through the regular season on a 23-game winning streak. As they knocked off one national power after another, the Crusaders began out-drawing the Boston Celtics.

In the NCAA Tournament, Holy Cross defeated Navy, City College of New York, and Oklahoma to claim the national title.

The following year, the champs had a new on-campus gymnasium.

DID YOU KNOW . . .
- Future Hall of Famer Bob Cousy played limited action in the big game. The freshman scored two points.
- The fans' favorite cheer for the Crusaders was "Choo-choo-rah-rah!"
- Because the Crusaders played a slick brand of give-and-go, newspapers gave them the nickname Fancy Pants A.C., which was a playful reference to the athletic-club teams of that era.

Homeless Dons

Another small Jesuit school, the 3,000-student University of San Francisco, had no campus gym in the 1950s. The Dons coach, Phil Woolpert, had to coax, wrangle, and finagle practice time for his squad at the parish hall, a neighborhood boys club, and nearby St. Ignatius High School where he once coached. Despite the lack of decent facilities, the Dons won back-to-back national championships in 1955 and 1956—including a then record 60-game winning streak.

Twin Wins

The City College of New York Beavers earned an enviable

record that can never be duplicated. They are the only team ever to win both the NCAA and NIT championship games in the same season.

They accomplished the feat by upsetting the same team twice, the No. 1 ranked Bradley University Braves of Peoria, Illinois.

It happened in 1950, the last year such a remarkable finish was possible. At the time, the NIT and NCAA were on equal terms and it was possible for teams to compete in both tournaments. Many did, but none had ever come close to accomplishing what CCNY did.

Bradley arrived at New York's Madison Square Garden, site of the NIT, with an outstanding 28–3 season record. As the top seed in the tourney, the Braves boasted a lineup of three All-American candidates—Paul Unruh, Gene "Squeaky" Melchiorre, and Billy Mann. Meanwhile, lightly regarded, unranked CCNY entered the tournament with a 17–5 record and a lineup consisting of one senior and four sophomores.

In the opening round, the Beavers recorded the first in a string of stunning upsets by thrashing San Francisco, the defending NIT champions. Then the Beavers pounded Kentucky, the NCAA defending champs, 89–50. It was the worst defeat for Adolph Rupp in his 42 years of coaching. (In the Kentucky locker room after the game, Rupp told his players, "I want to thank you boys. You get me elected Coach of the Year and then bring me up here and embarrass the hell out of me.") Next, CCNY decked Duquesne, 62–52, in the third round.

As expected, the Bradley Braves demolished their opposition en route to the finals against the surprising upstarts from the streets of New York.

In the championship game, Bradley led, 29–18, after 14 minutes and appeared in complete command. But, incredibly, the Braves didn't hit another field goal the rest of the half while CCNY struck back to cut the margin to 30–27. In the second half, the lead changed hands seven times before the Beavers pulled ahead and shocked most everyone by winning the NIT title game, 69–61.

The befuddled Braves hoped to salvage their pride in the NCAA Tournament, which CCNY had also entered. Both teams routed their foes and faced each other again in another title tilt at the Garden. The stage was set for the dramatic rematch—and Bradley's revenge. Instead, the finals turned into the another Big Apple Nightmare for the favored Braves.

Bradley and CCNY battled tooth-and-nail throughout the game. With 57 seconds left, the Beavers had a 69–63 lead, but the Braves scored five points in 20 seconds to bring them within a point of tying it up.

After CCNY turned the ball over on a wild pass, Bradley's Squeaky Melchiorre drove in the lane through heavy traffic for a layup that would have given his team the lead. The Braves were convinced he was hammered, but the refs didn't call any foul. CCNY center Irwin Dambrot blocked Melchiorre's shot and fired a long pass to teammate Norman Mager, whose uncontested basket sealed the Beavers's 71–68 victory and their second title in ten days.

The game gave CCNY the praiseworthy label of being the only team in history to win college basketball's two biggest tournaments in the same year.

Beginning with the 1950–51 season, the NCAA changed its selection system for post-season play, making it impossible for a team to play in both the NCAA and NIT tournaments. The change meant the CCNY Beavers will never have to share their mark of excellence with another team.

DID YOU KNOW . . .

• The cheer of the year in New York for Beavers fans: "Allagaroo-garoo-garah, allagaroo-garoo-garah; ee-yah, ee-yah; sis-boom-bah." According to school legend, an allagaroo was either a cross between an alligator and a kangaroo or a corruption of the French phrase "allez guerre" (which means "on to the war").

• Days after their team lost, angered Bradley fans headed to the Madison Theater in Peoria to see newsreel footage of the game, and they came away convinced Squeaky Melchiorre had been fouled on the crucial last-second play. The theater marquee read: "WAS SQUEAKY FOULED? YOU BE THE JUDGE."

Where the Madness Came from

Decades before the term March Madness referred to the NCAA Tournament, it was—and still is—used as the name for the Illinois High School Association's annual basketball tournament.

By the late 1930s, high school basketball in Illinois was big, especially the season-ending tournament that drew more than 900 schools and sell-out crowds. In 1939, Henry V. Porter, assistant executive secretary of the IHSA, wrote an essay in the organization's magazine, *Illinois*

Interscholastic, on the tourney's popularity. He called it "March Madness." The term was picked up by the state's newspapers, and soon "March Madness" became the popular name of the annual tournament.

In 1973, the IHSA began using the term officially in its programs and on its merchandise. Four years later, the organization enlisted veteran Chicago sportswriter and Big Ten basketball referee Jim Enright to write the official history book, *March Madness: The Story of High School Basketball in Illinois.*

The IHSA eventually received trademark status for the term "March Madness" and registered the trademark, "America's Original March Madness." A significant portion of the fees generated from the licensing of these trademarks is used to fund college scholarships for Illinois high school students.

March Madness was not used to describe the NCAA Tournament until 1982, when Brent Musburger, a CBS sportscaster at the time, used the term during the telecast of a tourney game. College basketball fans and the media have been using the name ever since.

Today, after a court case over the ownership of the term, March Madness is co-owned by the NCAA and IHSA through the March Madness Athletic Association.

The organizations share the income from the licensing fees.

"Know what I thought of our chances of getting to Seattle [for the 1952 Final Four]? I brought only two pair of socks and two pair of drawers [to Raleigh for the regionals]. I had to go out and buy underwear."
—St. John's coach Frank McGuire, whose team made it to the championship game, which it lost, 80–63, to Kansas

NEVER-SAY-DIE GAMES

Double Triple Overtimes

Never before or since has a team been pushed so hard to win the national championship as the North Carolina Tar Heels were. In the 1957 Final Four, they won back-to-back triple overtime games in the span of 24 hours.

The top-ranked 30–0 team took on the 16–8 Michigan State Spartans in the semifinal match-up in Kansas City. The upset-minded Spartans played North Carolina even throughout the game. With the score tied 58–58, Michigan State's Jack Quiggle heaved a 50-footer that went through the net as time expired, triggering jubilation among MSU's fans. But to their dismay—and the

Tar Heels' relief—the refs ruled the shot was released a split second after the horn.

In the first overtime period, Michigan State led, 64–62, with six seconds left and had Johnny Green at the foul line with a one-and-one, and a chance to ice the game. Green missed. North Carolina's Pete Brennan rebounded the ball, dribbled nearly the length of the floor and sank a 20-foot buzzer-beater to send the game into double OT.

"I knew at the end of that first overtime that Michigan State was done," Tar Heels coach Frank McGuire told reporters later.

Slowing down the action, each team managed to score only one basket in the next extra frame.

North Carolina star Lennie Rosenbluth, who ended up notching 29 points, opened the third overtime with a steal and layup to give UNC a 68–66 lead. Then, after Jack Quiggle tied the score for the Spartans, Rosenbluth put the Tar Heels ahead to stay with a long jumper. Teammate Tommy Kearns added a pair of free throws for a 72–68 advantage. Another Rosenbluth steal led to a layup and his team's final points as the worn-out Tar Heels outlasted the fatigued Spartans, 74–70.

The lead had changed hands 31 times and the score was tied 20 times.

The Tar Heels didn't have time to savor their victory or get much rest because the next night they took on 7-foot-1 Wilt Chamberlain and his Kansas Jayhawks. At the time, Wilt the Stilt was considered the most intimidating player in college basketball.

But the Tar Heels showed no ill effects from their exhausting triple overtime game, racing out to a 19–7 lead by hitting their first nine shots and settling for a 29–22 advantage at the break. In the second half, Kansas surged ahead, 44–41, and then sat on the ball without taking a shot for five minutes.

Things looked grim for UNC when Rosenbluth, who had scored 20 points, fouled out with 1:45 left in regulation. But KU's Gene Elstun missed the free throw. The Tar Heels then rallied for a 46–46 tie when Kearns sank two free throws in the final seconds, sending the game into overtime.

In the first OT, benches cleared after North Carolina's Pete Brennan clamped his arms around Chamberlain's waist and began to wrestle. Coach McGuire got in the melee and later claimed a Kansas assistant punched him in the stomach. The pro-Jayhawks crowd surged menacingly toward the court until police restored order. The fracas encompassed most of the action in the extra period because each team mustered only a lone basket.

The offense went to sleep in the second overtime as neither squad scored. UNC fans were squirming. Their team was dragging, their star was on the bench and the Tar Heels were about to enter their third OT for the second consecutive night. But North Carolina got its second, or rather third, wind and leaped out to a four-point lead on Kearns's basket and two free throws. Then Chamberlain completed a three-point play and Elstun sank two free throws to give Kansas a 53–52 lead with 20 seconds left.

In the waning seconds, Chamberlain blocked one desperation shot and then another. Tar Heels center Joe Quigg, who had been playing with four fouls for almost 30 minutes, drove the lane and was fouled with six seconds on the clock. Up until then no player in an NCAA title game had ever faced such pressure-packed free throws. If he made them, North Carolina would take the lead and probably win the championship. If he sank only one, the teams faced the likelihood of a fourth overtime. Miss them both and UNC's perfect season was over.

Surprisingly, McGuire called a time-out. Usually in that situation, it's the opposing coach who wants the time-out, hoping the extra minute gives the shooter more time to squirm. But McGuire wanted to assure Quigg, who made 72 percent of his free throws during the regular season, that he had confidence in him.

Quigg didn't disappoint his coach, teammates, or the North Carolina fans. He sank both foul shots. And then he capped it off by deflecting a pass meant for Chamberlain, denying the tall guy (who had scored 23 points) from taking the potential winning shot. Kearns picked up the batted ball and heaved it into the air as the buzzer sounded. The longest title game in NCAA history was finally over.

The exhausted Tar Heels were the undefeated national champions. And all it took was winning back-to-back triple overtime thrillers.

The Really Loooong Games

Talk about games that went on and on and on and on. The NCAA Tournament has seen two quadruple overtime knuckle-gnawers.

In the first round in 1956, Canisius College—a tiny unranked Jesuit school in Buffalo, N.Y.—went up against mighty North Carolina State, the second-ranked team in the country. The Wolfpack swaggered into New York showing off an impressive 24–3 record and expecting to swat the 17–6 Griffins. But this was the NCAA Tournament where anything can—and does—happen.

Canisius hung tough and wouldn't let N.C. State pull away. At the end of regulation, the score was knotted,

65–65. Both teams scored four points in the first overtime. In the second OT, the Wolfpack began pressing on the court—and in their minds—and scored only two points, as did the Griffins. Neither team could make a shot in the third extra period, but then they went on a scoring jag in the fourth OT.

N.C. State was clinging to a one-point lead when Fran Corcoran of Canisius took a shot with four seconds on the clock. The ball rattled through the rim, giving the Griffins a heart-stopping 79–78 upset victory. The shot that won the longest contest in tournament history was the only basket that Corcoran made all game.

***

Five years later, in 1961, the St. Joseph's University Hawks and the University of Utah Utes needed four overtimes in a battle for third place. (The NCAA eliminated the consolation game in the Final Four after the 1981 tourney.)

The Hawks held a 56–44 lead early in the second half, but Billy McGill, who scored 34 points, sparked a Utah comeback that gave the Utes a 78–77 lead with 5:24 to go. The game was tied four times in the final minutes and ended in regulation, 89–89.

Whether from pressure, exhaustion or excitement, Billy

Hoy of St. Joe's opened the first overtime by making a classic blunder. He drained a 15-footer directly off the tip—right into the Utah basket. The Hawks soon fell behind by four points, but they rallied to force another extra period with the score tied at 97–97.

In the second OT, each team garnered four points. At 101–101 entering the third overtime, both offenses kicked into gear. With the final seconds ticking off and the score 112–112, St. Joe's set up for the potential game-winning shot, but Utah batted the ball away. That meant a fourth extra period. This time, the Hawks pumped in 15 points and finally put the Utes away, 127–120.

As it turned out, it was all for naught. The Hawks' third-place win was stricken from the official record books because three St. Joe's players were implicated in a gambling scandal less than a month after the season ended.

LUCKY STIFFS

Before the La Salle Explorers left for Kansas City to play in the Final Four in 1954, the Philadelphia Chamber of Commerce presented shamrocks, specially flown in from Ireland, to senior guard Frank "Wacky" O'Hara. The good luck charms worked.

La Salle beat Penn State, 69–54, and then, with O'Hara directing the offense, ripped Bradley, 92–76, for the championship.

The Rambling Comeback

Things looked bleak for the Loyola Ramblers. Here it was, midway in the second half of the 1963 NCAA title game, and the two-time defending champion Cincinnati Bearcats were crushing the team from the small Chicago Jesuit school, 45–30.

Cincinnati had the game all but won. After all, it was the top defensive squad in the nation, holding opponents to an average of 53 points. And the Ramblers—the country's best offensive team, averaging 93 points per game—were making the Bearcats's job easy by missing 13 of their first 14 shots and managing a meager 21 points in the first half. Loyola's star player, senior Jerry Harkness, hadn't even scored a basket by then.

But while the complacent Bearcats eased up, the Ramblers didn't give up. Pressuring Cincinnati with a full-court press, Loyola fought its way to a stunning 60–58 overtime victory in one of the greatest comebacks ever in a title game.

Loyola, which played its home games in the cramped 2,000-seat Alumni Gym, was known for its "racehorse basketball." The Ramblers loved to fast break and press and score easy baskets and wear their opponents down. Coach George Ireland expected his players to run six-minute miles during training and to give 110 percent in his drill-instructor-style practices that were often tougher than the games.

The third-ranked Ramblers entered the tournament with an imposing 24–2 record. They annihilated Tennessee Tech, 111–42, in a record blowout. Then they dispatched Mississippi State, Illinois, and a strong 27–2 Duke squad to reach the finals against mighty 26–1 Cincinnati, the country's top team, which was gunning for a then-unprecedented third straight title.

The night before the game, which was played in Louisville's Freedom Hall, the Ramblers met in the hotel room of starters Les Hunter and Vic Rouse. "Rouse was the son of a preacher man and he was preaching about how we were going to win," Hunter recalled years later to Paul Kuharsky of the Nashville *Tennessean*. "He was going through all the motions of his dad, a Baptist minister. We were just doing the 'Amens' and everything, just really psyching ourselves up for the game. We didn't get any sleep that night. That may have thrown our timing off."

Whatever it was, the next evening Loyola couldn't find the basket with a search party and kept falling further and further behind. Harkness later admitted that all he could think about was not embarrassing his family and friends who were watching the ongoing beating on TV. At the half the Ramblers were down, 29–21.

Early in the second half, the lead grew. During a time-out, Hunter thought about the three-minute, 24-point barrage the Ramblers unleashed against Duke the previous game. Even though his team was shooting below 30 percent, he believed they were bound to get back on track.

"Every game there was a point, about three or four minutes, where we just took over, stole passes, blocked shots, got easy baskets," Hunter recalled. "In my mind I kept saying, 'When is that spurt going to come?'"

It came after Cincinnati tried to freeze the ball with about ten minutes left, passing up good shots to run time off the clock. Loyola seized the opportunity and attacked with a furious full-court press that rattled the tournament-tested champs. The smothering defense stole bad passes, stripped balls and caused Cincinnati to make other turnovers. The Bearcats had become so flustered they began missing their foul shots. And all the while, the Ramblers were finding their shooting touch during a dramatic late-game 22–8 run.

With the Bearcats up, 53–52, with 12 seconds left, Cincinnati's Larry Shingleton made the first of two free throws but missed the second. Hunter grabbed the rebound and fired an outlet pass to Ron Miller, who flipped it to Harkness for a game-tying basket. Five seconds remained, but the Bearcats were so shaken they failed to call time-out, and the buzzer sounded with the score deadlocked, 54–54.

In overtime, the teams traded baskets until it was 58–58 with over two minutes left. Then the Ramblers gambled by holding the ball, hoping to take the last shot.

As the final seconds ticked down, Harkness dribbled around looking for an opening but couldn't lose defender Ron Bonham, so he passed to Hunter, who tried a jump shot from the left side of the lane. The ball rolled off the rim directly into the hands of Rambler forward Vic Rouse, who jumped up and laid it in with two seconds left.

Loyola had just completed one of the most amazing comebacks in Final Four history to dethrone the defending champions and claim the title.

DID YOU KNOW . . .

- In a first that has never been duplicated, the Ramblers's five starters played every second of the game, including overtime. Meanwhile, the Bearcats used only one player off the bench.
- Loyola turned the ball over only three times while forcing Cincinnati into 16 miscues. The Ramblers shot just 27 percent, compared to the Bearcats's 49 percent.

DID YOU KNOW . . . (CONTINUED)

- The newspapers also carried a classic photo of a Loyola cheerleader on her knees at courtside, praying when her team was way behind. The girl whose prayers were answered was Coach George Ireland's daughter.

The Comeback Cats

On its way to claiming the 1998 title, the Kentucky Wildcats did what no other championship team had ever done before—rally from double-digit second-half deficits in each of its final three tournament games.

Being behind at the half was no big deal for the Wildcats. Been there; done that. Twelve times in the season, they trailed at intermission. Ten times they came back to win.

No wonder they were called the Comeback Cats.

Kentucky waltzed through its first three games of the tourney, winning by hefty double-digit margins. But after that, the Wildcats found themselves climbing their way out of one hole after another.

In the South Regional final in St. Petersburg, Florida, Kentucky was getting blown out by Duke, 69–52, with less than 12 minutes left in the game. It looked like the Blue Devils would win their fifth straight over Kentucky.

But the Cats didn't panic. Instead, they employed a withering full-court defense and began making their shots. Six minutes and a 19–3 run later, they had slashed that 17-point margin down to one, 72–71.

The Blue Devils fought back to build a 79–75 lead before Kentucky went on a 10–2 run—taking its first lead of the game at the 2:15 mark—and then held on for an oh-so-sweet 86–84 victory.

The following week, in the national semifinals at the Alamodome in San Antonio, the Wildcats once again fell behind by double-digits, this time to Stanford, 46–36, with 17:30 left in the game. But the Cats went on another one of their sprees and vaulted ahead for the first time in the game, 54–53. Neither team could pull away and at the end of regulation it was tied, 73–73. Kentucky scored the first five points in overtime and won, 86–85, which put it in the championship game for the third straight year.

In the title clash with Utah, the Comeback Cats were forced to live up to their reputation. Not surprisingly, they trailed at the half by double digits, 41–31. At the time, no team in NCAA history had ever overcome such a large halftime deficit in a championship game. Kentucky would be the first.

The team waited until it trailed 45–33 with 16 minutes left before making its move. The Utes began to run out of gas while the Wildcats, whose stamina was built on grueling 6 a.m. conditioning drills during the regular season, roared back. In the final five minutes, Utah failed to hit a basket in 11 attempts. Meanwhile, Kentucky sank nine of ten free throws down the stretch en route to a 78–69 triumph. It was the school's seventh NCAA championship and second in three years.

The Wildcats, who were out-rebounded 24–6 in the first half, limited the Utes to a miserable 29 percent shooting in the second half while grabbing 18 rebounds to Utah's 15.

"We've learned that if we keep our poise, continue to play hard and not give up, we can make good things happen," said backup guard Heshimu Evans, whose two three-pointers, a layup and a blocked shot sparked the decisive rally. "We're a fighting team—the Comeback Cats."

DID YOU KNOW . . .
- Utah coach Rick Majerus said after the game that his only plans were to attend the Kentucky Derby in May, where he expected to receive a warm welcome because Utah had lost to Kentucky for the third straight year in the NCAA Tournament. "People should be coming up and buying me stuff," he cracked.

Why Worry?

Duke was getting trounced in a 2001 national semifinal game against Maryland, 39–17, with less than seven minutes left in the first half when frustrated Coach Mike Krzyzweski called time-out and laced into his players.

"You're losing by so much, you can't play any worse," he told them. "So what are you worried about? Losing by forty? We're already losing by twenty-two, so will you just play?"

That seemed like a good idea to the Blue Devils. They returned to the court and, following their coach's advice, quit calling plays and just played the game. They broke into a devastating run as Mike Dunleavy Jr. hit three consecutive three-pointers in a 45-second span. For the third time that season against Maryland, the Blue Devils erased another double-digit deficit, surging ahead with less than seven minutes remaining in the game. Duke won going away, 95–84, and then drubbed Arizona, 82–72, for the championship.

The 22-point deficit was the largest that any team had overcome to win a Final Four game.

"We certainly have never gotten over that embarrassing defeat. It was a game that should have been ours. I have been kicking myself ever since."
—UCLA center Bill Walton, recalling the bitter 80–77 double-overtime loss to North Carolina State in the 1974 semifinals when the Bruins blew an 11-point second-half lead and a seven-point lead in the second extra period.

It Ain't Over 'til It's Over

In arguably the most amazing comeback in Elite Eight history, Illinois stormed back from 15 points down with less than four minutes remaining to steal an epic victory and advance to the 2005 Final Four.

Playing before a heavily partisan crowd at Allstate Arena in the Chicago suburb of Rosemont, the top-ranked Illini looked as if their 35–1 dream season was heading for an agonizing end. The Arizona Wildcats (30–6) had just gone on an 18–6 spree to take a commanding 75–60 lead with 4:04 left.

But the never-say-die Illini refused to quit.

"We just kept fighting," said guard Deron Williams. "We never gave up. It looked like the game was over. But it wasn't. I kept telling my teammates, 'We've got to keep going, keep playing. This game is not over. There's still some time. We can still get it [the lead] down, chip away.'

We ended up getting the momentum, the crowd got into it, and we were able to take the game over."

Firing up their defense, the Illini went on a rampage, stealing passes, hitting shots and denying Arizona a single field goal the rest of the way. Williams and Luther Head each sank a three-pointer and a layup and then Dee Brown drove the lane for a basket, chopping the lead to 80–72 with 1:03 left. It still seemed far-fetched that Illinois could actually pull it off, but the screaming orange-and-blue-clad crowd sensed a miracle in the making. Head drilled another three-pointer and then Brown stripped the ball, which was scooped up by Williams, who fed Brown for a basket to make it 80–77 with 45 seconds remaining. After Jack Ingram deflected a lob pass, Williams hit a three-pointer to tie it, 80–80, with 38 seconds to go.

The shrieks of joy from the delirious pro-Illini fans in the arena were so loud they were drowning out the jets taking off from nearby O'Hare Airport. "The crowd helped us so much," Williams said. "When we got back into the game, got the momentum, [the Arizona] players got rattled by that, and we were able to take the game."

Although shell-shocked, the Wildcats still had plenty of time to save themselves. They dribbled the clock down but failed to score on three shot attempts, the last of which was blocked by Head as time expired. What seemed an impossibility just a few minutes earlier was now a reality: The game was going into overtime because of Illinois's frantic, last-ditch 20–5 run.

With the help of two more three-point bombs from Williams in the extra period, the Illini hustled out to a 90–84 lead and then held on for an exhausting, improbable 90–89 triumph.

"I still don't know what happened," said a happily disbelieving Head, who scored 20 points and made four steals despite suffering a sore right hamstring.

Brown called it a miracle. "It's heart, man," he said. "It's just heart. The whole time I was saying, 'If it was meant to be, it was meant to be.' And I guess it was meant to be that we go to the Final Four."

In the raucous locker room, Illinois coach Bruce Weber kept shaking his head in wonder, uttering, "Just amazing."

On the other side, where the atmosphere was more somber than a wake, Arizona's Mustafa Shakur said, "Guys left and right on their team were hitting big buckets, left and right, left and right. It was just an unbelievable thing to lose a game that way."

Added Wildcats coach Lute Olson, "You look at it now [and] there are a lot of things that are going to force a lot of sleepless nights for everyone."

DID YOU KNOW . . .

- Illinois's next opponent was Louisville, which on the same day as the Illini's incredible win, launched its own amazing comeback. Rallying from a 20-point first-half deficit and a ten-point hole with five minutes left in the game, the Cardinals trimmed West Virginia, 93–85, in overtime. Louisville couldn't muster up another comeback in the national semifinals at St. Louis, though, and was creamed, 75–58, by Illinois.

- For the first time ever, three of the four games of the Elite Eight went into overtime in 2005. Besides the Illinois-Arizona and Louisville–West Virginia OT thrillers, Michigan State and Kentucky needed two extra periods. By making 11 straight free throws in the second overtime, MSU came out on top, 94–88.

- What made the MSU-KU game so memorable was the shot at the end of regulation. Down 75–72, Kentucky's Patrick Sparks released a desperation, double-clutching buzzer-beater from beyond the three-point line. The ball bounced on the rim four times before dropping through the net. Officials spent six minutes, 25 seconds reviewing the video to see if Sparks's foot was on the line. After having CBS blow up the image, the refs determined that his foot was a slim one-eighth inch behind the line, making the shot good and sending the game into overtime. "It seemed like that ball sat on the rim for a half hour and that's how long it seemed they reviewed it," said Michigan State coach Tom Izzo.

"If you lose a game in the Final Four, you'll feel worse than you ever felt in your life."
—Syracuse coach Jim Boeheim, before his team lost to Kentucky, 76–67, in the 1996 title game

IGNOBLE
INCIDENTS

The Pass to Notoriety

Fred Brown made one of the most errant passes ever in any NCAA championship game—and it couldn't have come at a more crucial moment.

With eight seconds left in the 1982 title game, the Georgetown Hoyas had the ball, but the North Carolina Tar Heels owned a 63–62 lead. Brown, Georgetown's usually reliable sophomore guard, rushed the ball upcourt, determined to get it to one of his teammates for the game-winning basket.

He saw that Sleepy Floyd was covered, as were Patrick Ewing and Ed Spriggs. "I should have called time-out, but

I decided to pass it to Eric Smith, who was on the right side of the lane," Brown recalled. "I thought I saw Smitty out of the corner of my eye. But it wasn't him."

No, it was North Carolina's James Worthy. Brown fired a perfect chest-high pass right into the hands of a happily surprised Worthy, who clutched the ball and then dribbled the other way until he was deliberately fouled with two seconds left. Worthy missed both free throws, but it didn't matter. Georgetown lost, 63–62.

Hoyas coach John Thompson summoned Brown toward the bench and gave him a big bear hug—a gesture that brought a lump in the throats of the crowd at the Louisiana Superdome in New Orleans.

To his credit, Brown owned up to his mistake after the game. He sat at his locker and politely answered every question that the throng of reporters asked him.

"Worthy didn't steal it—I gave it away," he said. "My peripheral vision is pretty good, but this time it failed me. It was only a split second. But that's all it takes to lose a game. I knew it was bad as soon as I let it go. If I'd had a rubber band, I would have yanked it back in. I had made so many similar passes throughout the game, and someone from my team was always there. But not that last time."

Although Brown never made an excuse, some believe his brain sprain was understandable. Up until that game, as the higher-seeded team in its region, Georgetown had worn white uniforms. But in the title game, North Carolina was in white. It was possible that in the heat of the moment, he caught a glimpse of the white uniform moving to the outside and threw it to that spot.

Thompson told reporters, "I feel bad for Fred. But he's a tough kid. We're not mad at Fred. And we don't feel like he lost the game."

Worthy said he was startled when Brown threw the ball to him. "I saw him fake the pass away [to Floyd]. He looked back and I just stood there. I thought he would throw it over my head. I was pretty surprised when it landed in my chest."

Remarkably calm, Brown said, "It was a great game. I loved playing it. I just wish the score was reversed at the end of the game. I hate to lose. Boy, I really hate it. But I can't let this affect my life. Coach Thompson told me after the game that I had won more games for him than I had lost. He said not to worry."

Many of the reporters surrounding Brown thanked him for answering their questions, and some shook his hand. "How can you be so composed?" a sportswriter asked him.

Brown replied, "This is part of growing up."

Putting the blunder behind him, Fred Brown persevered. Two years later, in the final game of his collegiate career, Brown became a champion when Georgetown flogged Houston, 84–75, for the national title. No one was happier than the senior guard.

When the last second ticked off the scoreboard, Coach Thompson, who had been quick to console Brown after his 1982 blunder, sought him out to hug first.

DID YOU KNOW . . .

• Dave Gavitt, 1982 tournament selection committee chairman, told the *Sporting News* about a light-hearted conversation he had with John Thompson over dinner a month after the game. "John says, 'I've gotten so much mail about that one vision of me with my arm around Freddie Brown. And you know, no one even knows what I said to him. I could have been saying, 'You stupid jerk.'"

• Fred Brown's bad pass wasn't the only reason Georgetown lost the 1982 title game. Consider what Hoyas center Patrick Ewing did in the early moments of the game: North Carolina's first four baskets were the result of goal-tending calls against Ewing.

DID YOU KNOW . . . (CONTINUED)

- Prior to this game, Tar Heels coach Dean Smith had taken his teams to the Final Four six times without a championship, prompting Georgetown fans to yell, "Choke, Dean, choke!"
- The game-winning shot—a 16-footer from the corner with 16 seconds left—was made by freshman Michael Jordan. He told reporters afterward that he had fantasized about that moment on the team bus on the way to the Superdome.

Time (Out) Constraints

The Michigan Wolverines never would have made it to the title games in 1992 and 1993 without the shooting, rebounding, and passing skills of Chris Webber, one of the Fab Five. As good as he was, however, Webber will forever live with the stigma of being the player who made a crucial gaffe in the waning seconds of the 1993 championship game.

He called a time-out that his team didn't have.

With a minute to play in the clash against North Carolina at the Louisiana Superdome, Michigan trailed, 72–67. But the Wolverines's Ray Jackson hit a basket and, following a Tar Heel turnover, Webber scored with 35 seconds left, cutting the lead to 72–71. Fifteen seconds later, Michigan fouled North Carolina forward Pat Sullivan who sank the front end of a one-and-one, but missed the second free throw.

Webber, who led his team in scoring and rebounding with 23 points and 11 boards, snared the rebound and headed up court. A basket would tie the game, a three-pointer would win it. He dribbled until he was near the corner in front of the Michigan bench. Covered by two Tar Heels and with no one to pass to and no open shot, Webber called a time-out with 11 seconds left.

To his horror, he realized that the Wolverines had no time-outs left, causing the refs to slap Michigan with a technical foul. North Carolina's top scorer, Donald Williams, stood alone at the free-throw line and calmly sank both shots for a 75–71 lead. Because of the technical, the Tar Heels got the ball out of bounds, so Williams was immediately fouled again. He made both those free throws to close out the scoring.

After the game, a dejected Webber told reporters, "I just called time-out. It was one we didn't have. It probably cost our team the game."

Michigan coach Steve Fisher said that during the team's final time-out with 45 seconds left, he thought he made it clear there were no more. "In the heat of the moment, strange things happen," Fisher said. "Chris said he heard someone hollering and calling for a time-out. It's an awful way to end the season."

Shortly before he became the first pick in the 1993 NBA draft after leaving college early, Webber said, "I'm not happy it [the time-out boner] happened. But I know it's going to help me in some way. It made me a man. It made me grow up a lot faster than if it hadn't happened."

DID YOU KNOW . . .

- Webber turned a negative into a positive. Knowing that he would always be remembered for the time-out that wasn't, he set up a charity foundation called Timeout. The organization helps youngsters in Detroit and Washington, D.C.
- Webber's father, Mayce, tried to make light of Chris's blunder by getting a vanity license plate that said "TIMEOUT."
- Before the 1992–93 season began, Tar Heels coach Dean Smith gave each player a photo of the Superdome with the caption, "North Carolina, 1993 NCAA Champions." He told his players to tape it where they would see it every day to remind them of their goal. The motivational trick obviously worked.

Bad Time

Officials with a bad sense of timing were responsible for one of the most controversial shots in tournament history. It happened in 1990 during Georgia Tech's Southeast Regional semifinal clash with the top-seeded Michigan State Spartans.

After a seesaw game, the Yellow Jackets were behind, 75–73, when freshman Kenny Anderson made what appeared to be an incredible game-winning three-pointer as time expired. Officials conferred and decided Anderson's foot was on the line, so the basket was changed to a two-pointer, sending the game into overtime.

However, replays showed that the jumper was released after the clock hit :00 but before the buzzer sounded. The basket should not have counted.

Nevertheless, the game continued in overtime, and Georgia Tech won, 81–80, on Dennis Scott's 12-foot hook shot. The Jackets prevailed in another squeaker, 93–91, over Minnesota to make it to the Final Four for the first time in school history before eventual champion University of Nevada–Las Vegas whipped them, 90–81.

Lost Time

It was the game that time forgot.

Officials befuddled by an apparent mechanical error

and an oversight by the timer created confusion in the climactic moments of one of the most important games of the season for both teams.

In the 1986 Midwest Regional semifinals in Kansas City, the Michigan State Spartans were nursing a 76–72 lead against the top-seeded 33–3 Kansas Jayhawks when KU's star player, Danny Manning, fouled out with 2:21 left. It appeared No. 5 seed MSU was about to knock off the team favored to go all the way.

After two Spartan free throws, Kansas put the ball in play and set up its offense. But then after an estimated 10 to 15 seconds had elapsed, an MSU player on the bench noticed that the official Kemper Arena clock hadn't started. Play was halted while the refs conferred. Over the vehement objections of Spartan coach Jud Heathcote, officials made no adjustment to the clock, claiming the rules didn't allow for them to use TV replays for timing issues. And that proved costly to Michigan State because those precious extra seconds were just enough time for Kansas to salvage the game.

With about a minute to play, the Spartans were still out in front, 80–74, but they had trouble protecting the lead. Only eight seconds remained when KU's Archie Marshall converted a tip-in to tie the score, 80–80, and ultimately push the game into overtime.

The Spartans were convinced that the basket shouldn't have counted because the game should have been over 10 to 15 seconds earlier—before the tying basket. Taking full advantage of the lucky break, KU rolled over MSU in overtime and won, 96–86. (The Jayhawks made it to the Final Four before Duke bumped them off, 71–67.)

As a result of the timing malfunction, the NCAA empowered its officials to utilize television replays to correct timing and scoring errors. But that's little consolation to Michigan State fans who will forever feel they were ripped off. Said Heathcote, "I thought it was a phantom game."

FASHIONISTAS?

The 1941 champion Wisconsin Badgers looked like giant versions of Munchkins in the Land of Oz. That's because their uniforms featured horizontally-striped red and white knee-high socks with red knee pads.

The La Salle Explorers, who won the title in 1954, were the first team to wear short-sleeved jerseys in the finals, which upset many purists of the game.

The 1977 Marquette Warriors were the first Final Four team to sport jerseys designed to be worn over their waist and not tucked in, causing critics to claim the team looked sloppy. The name Marquette was emblazoned at the bottom of the jerseys.

Absent-Minded

In back-to-back years, two key players were missing shortly before their championship games. One was sick and the other was lost.

Kentucky Wildcats coach Adolph Rupp was preparing his team for the 1951 title matchup with the Kansas State Wildcats at Williams Arena in Minneapolis when he realized that Cliff Hagan wasn't at the pre-game meeting. The 6-foot-4 sophomore was Rupp's prized sixth man, who could always be counted on to give his team the spark it needed.

Unfortunately, Hagan was sick, suffering from a head cold, a sore throat, and a fever. Still, Rupp expected Hagan to be with the team and was worried about him, so the coach ordered some of his players to search for their missing teammate.

They finally located him—relaxing in the hotel spa with a mudpack on his face. The spa treatment did little to make him feel any better, but the sick player joined the rest of the team at the arena. After examining Hagan, the team doctor told Rupp that the player was too ill to play.

Eight minutes into the game, Kentucky was trailing, 19–13, leaving Rupp fuming. He needed a spark. He needed Hagan. That was fine with the player, who was told to get into the game. Seconds later, Hagan tipped in a missed shot, giving his team a boost. He made five of six shots in the game and grabbed four rebounds as Kentucky claimed the championship, 68–58.

When asked by reporters later why he went against the doctor's advice and put Hagan into the game, Rupp replied, "I told the doctor, 'Hell, he's the right temperature to play.'"

***

The following year, the Kansas Jayhawks destroyed the St. John's Redmen, 80–63, at the Edmundson Pavilion in Seattle for the championship. But the victory didn't come without a scare for Kansas the night before when its star player, 6-foot-9 center Clyde Lovellette—the nation's leading scorer—went missing.

He didn't mean for that to happen. A Sigma Chi fraternity brother of Lovellette's was an ensign on a Coast Guard cutter that was anchored in Puget Sound. On the evening between the semis and the final game, the friend took Lovellette in a small boat out to the ship where they had dinner. By the time they left the cutter, thick fog had rolled in, and soon they were lost. It took a while, but they managed to get back to the ship, where Lovellette was forced to wait until the fog cleared. He finally returned to shore early in the morning of the big game and tried to tiptoe into his hotel room without being discovered.

"There was a newspaper reporter in the lobby of the hotel when I returned," Lovellette recalled years later. "He looked up, saw me, and looked back down at his paper. The story never broke in the paper. I had quite a fear of not being allowed to play against St. John's because not only had I missed curfew, but I got back extremely late. To this day, I don't even know if [Coach Phog Allen] ever knew about that incident."

Lovellette apparently didn't need much rest. He scored 33 points and snagged 17 rebounds in Kansas's rout of St. John's.

"This wasn't a game of X's and O's. It was one of complete . . . domination."
—Duke coach Mike Krzyzewski, after UNLV crushed the Blue Devils 103–73 for the 1990 national championship

One Thumb Down

Louisville Cardinals starter Wiley Brown was nearly thumbed out of the 1980 title game against UCLA in Indianapolis.

When Brown was four years old, he accidentally cut his right thumb with a sharp knife so severely that it had to be amputated, forcing him to eventually wear an artificial thumb. When he came to play basketball at Louisville, he wore three surgical gloves with the fingers cut out except for the thumb to hold the prosthesis in place. He usually got taped and had his hand prepared right after the pre-game meal.

The day before the game, Wiley accidentally left the prosthesis on the dining table after the team ate. Recalled Coach Denny Crum in *CBS Presents the Final Four*, edited by Matt Fulks: "When they got ready to tape him, he realized he wasn't wearing the thumb. He called the trainer. When they went back to where we ate, the table had already been cleaned off, and the thumb had been thrown out because they thought it was part of the garbage. To make matters worse, the garbage can was already emptied out back and into the big garbage container. There we were—the whole team—going through the garbage trying to find Wiley's prosthetic thumb. Luckily, they finally found it. The story is funny now, but at the time it wasn't because Brown played so much better with the artificial thumb. He could rebound and catch the ball a whole lot better."

With his fake thumb back in place, Wiley helped his team capture the title with a 59–54 victory over UCLA.

DID YOU KNOW . . .

- As Louisville's coach, Denny Crum had lost to his alma mater, UCLA, in three previous NCAA appearances— the semis in 1972 and 1975 and in the first round in 1977.
- Crum told reporters that at halftime of the 1980 game, when his team trailed 28–26, he accused his players of choking. "Then I apologized and told them I loved them. I realized they had been trying as hard as they could. I told them to loosen up and give it their best shot."

Lesson Learned

During his team's successful championship run in 1966, Texas Western coach Don Haskins insisted that his players refrain from starting any fights on the court—or face his wrath.

Everyone understood, and there were no scuffles throughout the tournament except one. "We had one knucklehead on our team who got in a fight during a game, and his name was Nevil Shed," recalled Shed in an interview with Milan Simonich of the Pittsburgh *Post-Gazette*.

The fracas happened during the first half of the Miners's second-round contest with the Cincinnati

Bearcats in Lubbock, Texas. While Shed was battling for position under the basket for a rebound, a Cincinnati player pulled Shed's shorts. Losing his cool, Shed wheeled around and took a wild swing at his opponent, barely grazing him. The players were separated and then the referees threw Shed out of the game.

Haskins was enraged to lose one of his players, especially one who had disregarded the coach's orders to avoid fighting. Angry, upset, and embarrassed, Shed started to walk off the court for the locker room in shame. But that wasn't good enough for Haskins. He demanded that Shed leave the building and told him not to bother getting on the team bus back to the hotel after the game.

Shed thought he was through playing basketball for Texas Western. But Haskins—who was in a much better frame of mind after the Miners had squeaked by the Bearcats, 78–76, in overtime—forgave him. Shed returned to the team to help Texas Western win the championship.

Oh, the Inhumanity of It All

Blowout, laugher, cakewalk. Call it what you will, but the greatest slaughter in NCAA Tournament history unfolded in 1963 when the Loyola Ramblers annihilated the Tennessee Tech Golden Eagles, 111–42.

For a Catholic school, Loyola didn't show much mercy

by ratcheting up a record 69-point margin of victory in the opening round of the Mideast Regional in Evanston, Illinois. Coach George Ireland and his boys apparently missed the catechism class on compassion when they dismembered the hapless Golden Eagles.

But then again, Tennessee Tech should shoulder some of the blame for the debacle, considering it set a record, too—in futility. The team holds the all-time lowest field goal percentage in an early-round game, shooting a paltry 22 percent (18-for-82) from the field.

The 16–7 Golden Eagles, the Ohio Valley Conference title-holders, were clearly overmatched against the 24–2 Ramblers, who considered their foes nothing more than a bunch of gym rats—the first victims on the road to Loyola's eventual national championship. Five minutes into the game, the outcome was not in doubt. But for some reason Ireland played his starters for virtually the entire time, and they were unrelenting.

It was bad enough getting beaten, but to get trounced so appallingly made Tennessee Tech coach Johnny Oldham stew for a few years. Oldham, who had taken his team to the Big Dance twice in the nine years he coached there, was hoping for a chance to get even. He finally did three years later, after landing the head coaching job at Western Kentucky, his alma mater.

As luck would have it, the Hilltoppers, who had a notable 23–2 record but were unranked and ignored by the media, faced off against the fourth-ranked 22–2 Ramblers in the opening round of the Midwest Regional in Kent, Ohio. The Western Kentucky players were out to avenge the record-setting drubbing their coach had suffered at the hands of Ireland and his Loyola bullies

Recalled Western Kentucky center Steve Cunningham in an interview on hilltopperhaven.com: "We had a chip on our shoulder [on behalf of Coach Oldham] because we knew what happened in the Loyola game. Ireland just poured it on and didn't take his starters out the whole ballgame." So the Hilltoppers were charged up and focused on giving the Ramblers a taste of their own medicine.

"They [the media] kept touting about the great full-court press that Loyola had," said Cunningham, adding that Western Kentucky turned the tables. "To start the ball game, I don't think Loyola made it across the half-court line for like the first six trips. We stole the ball or got the ball back or they made a turnover and we jumped out to a quick lead."

When it was over the Hilltoppers had hammered the highly favored Ramblers, 105–86. The 19-point margin of victory didn't come close to matching what Loyola had done to Oldham's former team, but it was still the worst beating the school had ever suffered in an NCAA Tournament game. "I think a lot of it was revenge, I really do," said Cunningham.

Years later, Oldham called it "one of my biggest wins ever." Oldham, who coached for 16 years and compiled an outstanding 260-123 record, including a third-place finish for Western Kentucky in 1971, added with a smile, "It was a little payback."

And the Band Played On

The Prairie View Panthers's one and only game in an NCAA Tournament turned into an inglorious affair—the second-worst defeat ever in the event's history. They achieved their moment of ignominy in the opener of the 1998 Midwest Regional in Oklahoma City when Kansas demolished them, 110–52.

The small, venerable Texas school seldom got any national press (not counting the stories later that year when its football team finally won to snap a record-setting 80-game losing streak). Prairie View, whose basketball program budget was chump change compared to the major powerhouses, had received an automatic bid to the Big Dance by upsetting Texas Southern, 59–57, to win the Southwestern Athletic Conference tournament. The players celebrated their victory by breaking into a step dance, which they called "Hoop Phi Hoop."

So what if the Panthers brought with them an unremarkable 13-16 record and were the 14th team in tournament history to enter with a losing mark? So what if they had to play the top-seeded Kansas Jayhawks, who were ranked second in the nation and sported a 35-3 record? So what if a No. 16 seed like Prairie View had never, ever won a tournament game?

"If we win, we're going to party," player Sylvester Lilly told the press. "If we lose, we're going to party."

For a team hoping to be a Cinderella, it chose an ominous departure time for its eight-hour bus trip to Oklahoma City—midnight. As for the game, it was no contest. The Jayhawks raced out to a 20–5 lead and rested at the half, ahead—make that way, *way* ahead—60–24.

Nevertheless, Prairie View got a standing ovation. Only it was for its renowned band, the Marching Storm, and the Black Foxxes, the school's energetic majorettes. With their animated, high-stepping showmanship, they wowed the crowd at halftime.

On the court, things didn't get much better for the Panthers, even after Kansas coach Roy Williams pulled his starters early in the second half. The deficit kept growing until mercifully time ran out before the Jayhawks could seriously challenge Loyola's record for ruthlessness.

After the rout, Williams was asked about the disparity between the two teams. His reply: "I'm not trying to put them down. I love their enthusiasm, but we had more weapons. We are more gifted than they are."

DID YOU KNOW . . .

• You would think that after winning a game by the second largest margin in tournament history, Kansas would be primed to barrel its way to the championship. Nope. In its very next outing, KU fell to No. 8 seed Rhode Island, 80–75.

SLEEPLESS IN MARYLAND

Among the reasons why Princeton lost to Michigan in the semifinals of the 1965 NCAA Tournament was the sleeping arrangements at the team's hotel.

At least that's what star Bill Bradley said.

The night before the Michigan game, the Princeton squad flew from New Jersey to College Park, Maryland, site of the Final Four. "When we checked into a motel—I think it was a Howard Johnson—my roommate and I discovered there were no beds," Bradley recalled. "All we had were pullout sofas. That's what they had us sleeping on. We thought, 'Here we are in the finals, and they can't

> *even give us a reasonable bed.'"*
>
> *Despite a restless night, Bradley scored 29 points the next day, but his bleary-eyed teammates couldn't keep up with the Michigan Wolverines and lost, 93–76.*

Shooting Blanks

The Kentucky Wildcats's shooting performance in the second half of the 1984 national semifinals against the Georgetown Hoyas was truly offensive—as in pathetic.

The Big Blue-hoo tallied just 11 points.

Not one Kentucky starter made a field goal, while the rest of the team was a shameful 3-of-33 from the floor. Astoundingly, the Wildcats failed to score a single point for the first nine minutes and 56 seconds of the half.

Needless to say, Kentucky lost, 53–40.

When the top-seeded Wildcats arrived at Seattle's Kingdome for the Final Four, they felt good about their chances. On their way to a 29-4 record, they were shooting at better than 52 percent. However, Georgetown brought to town its lofty 32-3 mark, No. 1 ranking, 7-foot All-American center Patrick Ewing, and a patent on an ironclad defense.

Early on, Kentucky gave no hint that its offense would play as if it were blindfolded. By making 50 percent of their field-goal attempts, the Wildcats built a 29–22 halftime bulge over Georgetown. The second half was another story, seemingly another team—the Gang that Couldn't Shoot Straight. The Wildcats missed their first 11 shots, then made just one of their next 11 as Georgetown's pressing defense forced turnovers and poor shots. While keeping them scoreless for nearly ten minutes, the Hoyas tallied 12 points and slowly pulled away for the victory.

"We like to tease our enemies, make them happy and think they will blow us out," said Georgetown coach John Thompson, whose team went on to beat Houston, 84–75, for the title. "Then we come back."

The Wildcats made only 24.5 percent of their shots overall, and an unbelievably pitiful 9 percent in the second half. The 40 points were the fewest by any team in the Final Four since 1949, when Kentucky defeated Oklahoma State, 46–36, in the championship game. The 11 second-half points is a record likely to live in infamy.

Kentucky coach Joe B. Hall, who tossed his rolled-up program over his shoulder in exasperation with four minutes to play, told reporters after the game, "What happened was totally beyond me. I've never seen a team shoot as bad as we did today. I can't explain it. There had to be some electronic device sending out sounds around the basket."

No to No. 1

Being seeded No. 1 in the NCAA Tournament was a curse for the DePaul Blue Demons in the early 1980s.

For three straight years, they held the top seed in their region, and possessed an awesome combined record of 59–3. Yet, all three times they were bounced from the tourney in the opening round.

In 1980, the Blue Demons, featuring future NBA star Mark Aguirre, were ranked No. 1 in the nation and had a No. 1 seed, but in their first game in the tournament, they fell to No. 8 seed UCLA, 77–71.

The following year, No. 1 seed DePaul faced a No. 9 seed, lowly-regarded St. Joseph's. The Blue Demons, who were nursing a seven-point lead in the second half, failed to score a point in the last six minutes of the game and lost, 49–48.

Then in 1982, when No. 1 seed DePaul was the second-ranked team in the nation, it was knocked off by No. 8 seed Boston College, 82–75.

Interestingly, in 1979, when DePaul was the No. 2 seed, it made it all the way to the Final Four before losing a squeaker to Indiana State, 76–74.

"We'll be in a swordfight with a pocketknife."
—Campbell University coach Billy Lee before his No. 16 seed Fighting
Camels were thrashed, 82-56, in 1992 by top-seed and eventual cham-
pion Duke

PRESSURE COOKER MOMENTS

Dash to Glory

During March Madness, the pressure in the final moments of a tight game can squeeze a player beyond the breaking point or forge him into a hero.

For example, Danny Ainge was a great college player, an NBA star, and a major league baseball player. But what he's most famous for in the eyes of hoops fans is his incredible last-second, coast-to-coast dash through the Notre Dame defense to score the winning basket in the 1981 East Regional semifinals.

The No. 6 seed Brigham Young Cougars were 24-7 when they went up against the 23-5 Notre Dame Fighting

Irish, the No. 3 seed and seventh-ranked team in the nation.

The game, played at the Omni in Atlanta, was a tight defensive struggle. Brigham Young was clinging to a 49–48 lead in the waning seconds when Notre Dame's Kelly Tripucka hit a clutch shot from deep in the corner with eight seconds left, putting his team in the lead.

After a Cougar time-out, Ainge wowed the crowd with his signature moment. Taking the inbounds pass from under the Notre Dame basket, he deftly and swiftly dribbled his way through all five defenders from one end of the court to the other and laid the ball in the basket a second before the buzzer, giving BYU a dramatic 51–50 victory. The win put the Cougars into the Elite Eight and sent the favored Fighting Irish home.

"He did it just like I told him to," Coach Frank Arnold joked later.

Glowed the *New York Times* at the time, "Ainge's dash to victory will stand as one of the finest plays of its type in NCAA Tournament history. Speed, mobility, ball-handling, balance and shooting—all the talents of a fine basketball player—were displayed in that maneuver by the 6-foot-5-inch guard."

Two days later, Virginia ended BYU's dreams with a stinging 74–60 defeat of the Cougars. Easing the pain of the loss, Ainge was named National Collegiate Player of the Year.

In 2003, when BYU honored Ainge and retired his uniform number, he said he knows he'll always be remembered for that moment. "Everywhere I go, even today, people still bring that up . . . That's the one that people remember the most, and it certainly was a highlight, without question."

* * *

Twenty-four years later, UCLA's Tyus Edney duplicated Ainge's dazzler. Edney drove the length of the court in less than five seconds and hit a short bank shot at the buzzer to beat Missouri, 75–74, in the second round of the 1995 West Regional.

The 5-foot-10, 152-pound guard, known for his late game heroics, had helped his team earn a No. 1 seed and the top ranking in the national polls. Although UCLA was favored over No. 8 seed Missouri, the Tigers scored with 4.8 seconds left on the clock to go up, 74–73.

The Bruins called time-out, and, in the huddle, Coach Jim Harrick called on his go-to guy, Tyus Edney. In practice, UCLA had a drill in which the players were required to dribble full court against a defender in six seconds or less. Edney had done it in less than five seconds. But that was in practice; this was a must-win game.

Edney, who had seen tape of Danny Ainge's 1981 dash to glory, felt confident. When play resumed, Cameron Dollar inbounded the ball to Edney, who took off up the left sideline. He lost his defender with a nifty left-handed, behind-the-back move. As Edney dribbled up the floor, the Missouri defenders—trying desperately to avoid fouling him—moved into his path and then stood still, not touching him nor reaching for the ball. They figured there was no way he could make it to the basket in time. They figured wrong.

Edney weaved around each defender and made it all the way to the lane, where he put up a five-foot baby hook shot over two defenders that kissed off the backboard and through the hoop as time expired, giving UCLA a breathtaking 75–74 victory.

Thanks to Edney's heroics, UCLA was able to move on in the tournament. The Bruins won the next four games to capture their 11th national championship.

"How much better can you feel when you feel great?"
—North Carolina coach Roy Williams, after his team toppled Illinois, 75–70, for the 2005 title

Passing Fancy

When it comes to memorable buzzer-beaters in tournament history, the shooter doesn't deserve all the credit. Kudos also belongs to the player who got the ball to him —especially when it requires a last-second, coast-to-coast pass.

In one of the greatest games ever played—Duke's 104–103 overtime heart-stopper over Kentucky in the 1992 East Regional final—a perfectly-executed 75-foot pass from Grant Hill allowed Christian Laettner to bury the game-winner as time expired.

In the epic struggle at the Spectrum in Philadelphia, the two teams combined to make 61 percent of their shots from the field. Momentum shifted back and forth. When Kentucky's Sean Woods banked a running hook shot over Laettner's outstretched hands to give the Wildcats a 103–102 lead with 2.1 seconds left, Duke's Bobby Hurley called time-out. Only 1.8 seconds remained on the clock. The team would have to go the length of the court and score in less than two seconds—a seemingly impossible task. It was pretty obvious the Blue Devils had lost the game and their chance to defend their title.

But in the huddle, Duke coach Mike Krzyzewski looked at his players and declared, "We're going to win." Once he saw in their eyes that they believed him, he drew up the play that will live in basketball lore.

"Whether you completely believe it or not, you have to have the expression on your face and the words in your mouth that we're going to get a good shot to win," he told reporters later.

From under Kentucky's basket, Hill hurled the ball 75 feet dead-on to Laettner, who had moved to the top of the key. Interestingly, Kentucky coach Rick Pitino had decided not to put any pressure on Hill. Instead, he had John Pelphrey and Deron Feldhaus double-team Laettner, who had been a perfect nine-for-nine from the floor. Pelphrey tried to intercept the pass but he missed. With his back to the basket, Laettner caught the ball and was lightly bumped by Pelphrey, who backed away, not wanting to risk a foul. Feldhaus also kept his distance.

Laettner faked to his right, dribbled once, turned to his left and launched a high, arcing shot four-tenths of a second before the buzzer sounded. It was good the instant it left his hand.

Grant Hill chased after Laettner, who was running around the court until he was mobbed by his delirious teammates. Duke player Thomas Hill was so shocked by such good fortune that he remained motionless and then sobbed as hard as a Death Row inmate who had just received an eleventh-hour reprieve.

Emotions spun to the depths of despair on the Kentucky side. Would-have-been-hero Sean Woods lay sprawled on the floor in agony. Pelphrey put his hands to his hair in shock. Wildcats walked off the floor like zombies, their minds and hearts void of any life. Even 30 minutes after the game, Pitino couldn't talk other than mumble, "My mind is in a total fog."

The Blue Devils next beat Indiana and Michigan for their second straight title. They never would have repeated as champs if Laettner hadn't hit the game-winning shot off a perfect floor-length pass from Grant Hill.

DID YOU KNOW . . .

- Krzyzewski showed remarkable class immediately after the classic battle. He consoled Wildcats player Richie Farmer, then went over to legendary Kentucky radio broadcaster Cawood Ledford, who was calling his final Kentucky game. As Ledford was signing off, Krzyzewski asked for his headset, put it on and over the air he spoke directly to the Wildcats fans and expressed his admiration for their team.

Passing Fancy #2

In a 1977 semifinal match-up between the Marquette Warriors and University of North Carolina–Charlotte 49ers, the score was tied with three seconds left in the game.

Before inbounding the ball under the 49ers's basket, the Warriors called time-out. Marquette coach Al McGuire strolled down court, peering up at Atlanta's Omni clock. He wasn't checking the score. "He wanted to see if I would hit the clock with a full-court pass, if the clock was too low," his star Butch Lee recalled years later. "He decided it was okay and said to me, 'Just let it go.'"

Lee fired a long pass to the other end of the court. The 49ers's Cedric "Cornbread" Maxwell leaped to intercept it, but the ball grazed his fingertips and landed in the hands of Lee's teammate Jerome Whitehead. The 6-foot-l0 junior center whirled, took one step toward the basket, and laid it in as time expired.

But there was some question about whether he beat the clock. Coaches, referees, and players alike crowded around the official timekeeper for the verdict. TV replays appeared to show that the ball left Whitehead's hands less than a second before the buzzer sounded. The shot counted. Marquette won and went on to capture the title two days later.

Passing Fancy #3

In the 1990 East Regional semifinals at East Rutherford, New Jersey, the 17th-ranked Clemson Tigers held a 70–69 lead over the third-ranked Connecticut Huskies with one second left in the game and a time-out on the floor.

"What I remember most is how calm Coach [Jim Calhoun] was," UConn player Steve Pikiell recalled. "We're down one with one second to go and we're thinking, 'We're going to win.' Coach was the calming influence. He diagrammed a play called 'Home Run.' We ran it every day in practice."

The play called for Scott Burrell to throw a 90-foot precision heave from virtually one end of the 94-foot court to the other. Burrell was certainly the man for the job. He had been recruited by colleges for both baseball and basketball, and would later play in the minor leagues in the Toronto Blue Jays farm system. "Scott always did the throwing," said Pikiell. "He was a tremendous athlete with a great arm."

When play resumed in the Clemson game, Burrell flung a perfect court-length pass to teammate Tate George, who caught it, turned, and sank the game-winning shot at the buzzer for a spectacular 71–70 Huskies victory.

It was difficult for Clemson fans to fathom how, with one second on the clock, George had sufficient time to receive a full-court pass, come down, square up and get off a winning jumper from the right baseline. But the refs said the shot counted, sending UConn to the Elite Eight.

DID YOU KNOW . . .

• Ironically, two days later, UConn was defeated on a buzzer-beater after Tate George lost the ball off his foot with 2.5 seconds left in the East Regional final. It was just enough time for Duke's Christian Laettner to toss in the game-winner as time expired, sending the Blue Devils to the Final Four with a 79–78 overtime triumph. (Many believe Laettner's winning shot was even more difficult than the one he sank against Kentucky two years later.).

Passing Fancy #4

Another player with major league baseball potential made a last-second throw that triggered one of the most memorable plays in NCAA Tournament history, giving the Valparaiso Crusaders a stunning 70–69 upset victory over the Mississippi Rebels in the opening round of the 1998 Midwest Regional in Oklahoma City.

The No. 13 seed Crusaders trailed the No. 4 seed

Rebels, 69–68, when Valparaiso called a time-out with only 2.5 seconds left in the game. Crusaders coach Homer Drew told his team to execute the "Pacer," a play named after one in the playbook of the NBA's Indiana Pacers. Guard Bryce Drew, the coach's son, always wondered why it was run so often in practice without being used in a game. Now he understood.

When play resumed, Jamie Sykes, an outfield prospect who was late for spring training with the Arizona Diamondbacks because of the tourney, was under the Rebels' basket. With a defender in his face, he hurled a baseball-like throw past mid-court to teammate Bill Jenkins, who leaped between two Mississippi players and delivered a perfect touch pass to Drew on the right wing. Drew had been left alone outside the three-point line when defenders converged on Jenkins. From 22 feet, Drew calmly drilled a leaning, game-winning three-pointer at the buzzer in what has become known in Valpo-land as "The Shot." But it all started with "The Pass."

DID YOU KNOW . . .

• The play won the 1998 ESPY Award, given by ESPN, as the "Play of the Year."

DID YOU KNOW . . . (CONTINUED)

• Drew Bryce said a Valparaiso alumnus was listening to the game in his car while driving on the Interstate somewhere between Detroit and Chicago when Drew made the winning shot. The man pulled over and got out of the car so he could jump and shout.

• Homer Bryce received congratulatory faxes from Japan, Hong Kong, and Germany. Another alumnus sent the front page of an Israeli newspaper that featured Valparaiso's upset prominently.

"We're going to shine all day, all night. Please don't be mad at us if we don't do a little homework the next couple of weeks."
—Florida star Joakim Noah, after the Gators chomped UCLA, 73–57, for the 2006 title

The Smart Shot
It's eerie how history can repeat itself in a championship game.

For example, in the 1982 final at the Louisiana Superdome, Michael Jordan sank a 16-foot baseline jumper from the left side with 16 seconds remaining to give North Carolina a spine-tingling 63–62 victory over Georgetown.

Five years later, in the 1987 final in the same arena, Keith Smart, from nearly the same spot on the floor, sank a 16-foot baseline jumper with five seconds remaining to give Indiana a riveting 74–73 triumph over Syracuse.

Smart wore jersey number 23—the same as Jordan did.

Before hitting the clutch shot, Smart had carried the Hoosiers down the stretch, scoring 12 of Indiana's final 15 points. He finished the night with 21 points, of which 17 came after intermission.

Smart had a slow start, he admitted, because he was suffering from title game nerves that had kept him up much of the night. At halftime, he recalled, "Everyone — Coach [Bobby] Knight, the other coaches, my teammates, the doctors—told me to settle down and play."

In the second half, the Orangemen shut down Indiana's leading scorer, Steve Alford, so Smart got more involved in the offense by penetrating, dishing off passes, and taking shots.

He took complete charge in the final minute. Syracuse was up, 73–70, when Smart grabbed a rebound and then scored with 30 seconds left to cut the margin to 73–72. Then on the inbounds play, he deliberately fouled freshman Derrick Coleman, who missed the front end of a one-and-one.

Indiana got the rebound and, with Smart directing the

offense, held for the last shot. High scorer Steve Alford (23 points) was covered, so Smart passed to Daryl Thomas (20 points) with ten seconds left. But Thomas didn't have a clear shot, so he kicked it back to Smart, who then took the title-winning jumper with five seconds on the clock. "The only thing that surprised me was that I went up for the shot and that it went in," he said. "That was the biggest surprise of all."

As if scoring the go-ahead basket weren't enough, Smart then intercepted a desperation floor-length Syracuse pass as time expired and hurled the ball into the red sea of Hoosier fans. Moments later, he was carried around the floor by his celebrating teammates.

Even in his wildest dreams, Smart never conjured up anything like this. The last time Smart, a Baton Rouge native, had been in the Superdome, he was with his fellow Boy Scouts, who were acting as ushers at a football game. As a high school senior, he was only 5-foot-7 but was the starting guard until he broke his wrist in the third game of the season. When Smart received only one recruiting letter from college, his high school coach talked William Penn College in Iowa into taking the player sight unseen. But before he could enroll, Smart again broke his wrist, this time in a motorcycle accident, and the scholarship offer was withdrawn. "Guys with a broken arm and dumb enough to ride motorcycles aren't much in demand," Indiana coach Bobby Knight once said.

But Smart claimed the motorcycle accident was the best thing that could have happened to him. He eventually played two years at Garden City (Kansas) Community College, where he flourished and grew to 6-foot-1 and caught the eye of several top coaches, including Knight, who for years had been adverse to even consider junior college transfers. But because the coach wasn't pleased with the high school talent pool, he brought in Smart and another junior college transfer, Dean Garrett.

The moves paid off big time because those two transfers were in the starting lineup for the championship game. Garrett scored ten points and snared ten rebounds, while Smart was named the tournament's Most Outstanding Player.

DID YOU KNOW . . .
• The championship game was the first time that Smart's father ever saw him play college basketball. "I'm glad my father was here," Smart said. "I think he probably liked that ending."

Pressure Points

In the do-or-die NCAA Tournament, one botched layup or one errant pass in the final seconds can cost a team everything it has worked so hard to achieve. Perhaps nowhere is the crushing pressure more intense than at the free-throw line with the game hanging in the balance. The player is all alone, the focal point of every breathing soul in the arena; the target of taunts from every opposing fan; the hope of every teammate and supporter.

Make it and he's a hero. Miss it and he's the goat. Among fans, he will either be famous for the rest of his life—or infamous.

How's this for pressure? You're at the foul line with three seconds left in overtime in the championship game and your team is trailing by one. Fans in more than 19 million households are glued to their TV sets—not to mention the 38,000 spectators in the arena—waiting to see what you're going to do. That was the palm-sweating situation for Michigan's Rumeal Robinson.

His moment of truth and tension came at the end of the 1989 title game in Seattle's Kingdome. The Seton Hall Pirates had the ball and a 79–78 lead with seven seconds left when Michigan's Glenn Rice picked off an air ball and passed to Robinson. Wolverines coach Steve Fisher earlier had told Robinson not to call a time-out, no matter what happened on the Pirates's possession. So Robinson dribbled the length of the court and penetrated down the middle. With three seconds to go, he was fouled by Seton Hall guard Gerald Greene.

"I didn't want to put the burden on anyone else's shoulders," Robinson said after the game. "I've been hiding on last-second shots. I decided if anyone took it, I wanted to be the one. I was either going to shoot or get fouled."

Robinson, a 64-percent foul shooter, stepped to the line for a one-and-one. He had to make the first one or it was all over. Before he had a chance to shoot, Seton Hall called time-out, hoping to rattle him.

When the teams returned to the court, Robinson eyed the basket as the Pirate fans screamed and the Wolverine fans held their breath. He swished the first one to tie the game. Confident, he raised his right arm and embraced teammate Mike Griffin. Then Robinson swished the second one to win it, 80–79.

Robinson's steely backbone was strengthened by a tough childhood. He was a 12-year-old street urchin after his mother deserted him following their move from Jamaica to Cambridge, Massachusetts. "Somewhere along the line I think I was blessed," he told reporters. "I feel no bitterness. I have not been cheated. I do not know why my mother did not want me. I do not know why my biological father died the day before I was to meet him. But I also do not know why I was so lucky to find my adoptive parents. It is not so much bad luck or good luck. It is . . . only how it is . . . how God wants it.

"It is a childhood dream to do something like this. You cherish the good times, but where I have come from, you remember the hard times."

Asked how he felt at the foul line, he replied, "It was a little cockiness, but mostly confidence. You have to believe you're going to make them because if you don't, you won't."

What he probably didn't realize at the time was the free throws were worth about $300,000—the amount that was coming to Michigan for winning the title.

* * *

When junior Christian Laettner stood at the free-throw line in the final seconds of the 1991 national semifinals, he carried the weight of Duke history on his shoulders. Eight times, the Blue Devils had reached the Final Four and eight times they had come away empty-handed.

And now the score was tied, 77–77, with undefeated defending champion UNLV—a team that had returned four starters from the previous year when it embarrassed Duke, 103–73, in the worst shellacking ever in a tournament title game.

The clock showed 12.7 seconds remaining when Laettner faced a one-and-one while the 45,000-plus fans at the Hoosier Dome wondered if he could handle the pressure. They also wondered if he had any gas left in the tank after playing every second of the game, which had 17 ties and 25 lead changes.

Laettner showed them. He drained both foul shots to give the Blue Devils a milestone 79–77 victory that catapulted them to the championship game, which they won, 72–65, over Kansas. Laettner, by the way, was 12-for-12 from the free-throw line in that contest.

* * *

In the opener of the 1987 playoffs, the No. 14 seed Austin Peay Governors were losing, 67–66, to third-seeded Illinois when the fate of the game rested in the hands of Austin Peay's Tony Raye. He had just been fouled with two seconds on the clock.

Everyone in the Birmingham, Alabama, arena had the same questions: Would he give the Governors an incredible upset victory by making both foul shots? Would he send the game into overtime by hitting only one of them? Or would he let the heavily favored Illini escape with a one-point win by clanking both free throws? After Illinois's obligatory time-out to play with his mind, Raye answered all those questions by coolly sinking both his shots for a 68–67 upset.

* * *

Twelve years later, another No. 14–over–No. 3–seed upset concluded with two pressure-packed late-game free throws. Harold "The Show" Arceneaux tossed in two foul shots with 13 seconds left to cap a spectacular 36-point performance as his Weber State Wildcats upset North Carolina, 76–74, in the opening round of the 1999 play-offs. It was the first time in 19 years that the Tar Heels had lost an opener. (Weber State players reportedly received phone calls as late as 3 a.m. from Duke and Clemson fans congratulating them for knocking out their ACC rival.)

* * *

With Connecticut up, 72–71, and only 11 seconds left, Caron Butler was fouled on a three-point attempt and calmly buried all three foul shots for a four-point cushion over North Carolina State in the second round of the 2002 East Regional. But then N.C. State's Ilian Evtimov nailed a three-pointer to slice the lead back to one. Butler was fouled again with three seconds remaining, and sank both free throws for the winning margin. By hitting five of five foul shots in the final 11 seconds, Butler secured the Huskies's 77–74 victory.

* * *

In a 2006 opening round game, No. 4 seed Boston College was desperately trying to catch up to surprising Pacific, a No. 13 seed, in overtime. The Eagles had been down by six in the extra period but with 4.3 seconds left, they were within two when their star, Craig Smith, was fouled. He needed to sink both free throws to force a second overtime or suffer elimination. Smith, a 66 percent shooter from the line, tossed them both in for a 74–74 tie. Then, in the second OT, Boston College reeled off 14 points to Pacific's two for a hard-fought 88–76 triumph.

The Uncharitable Charity Linee

For many players in the NCAA Tournament, the charity

line is anything but charitable at crunch time. They go to the foul line with strong nerves, but they leave with weak knees.

It can happen to the best of them.

In a 1975 semifinal game against the UCLA Bruins, Louisville Cardinals ball-handling specialist and free-throw marksman Terry Howard was fouled with 20 seconds left in overtime and his team ahead, 74–73. The senior stepped to the charity stripe with a one-and-one. There was a good chance he would ice the game because he had not missed a free throw in 28 attempts all season.

He picked a terrible time to miss his first. The ball spun around the rim and out. UCLA grabbed the rebound and, with two seconds left, Richard Washington drilled a seven-footer for the win that put the Bruins into the title game.

* * *

In its opening round game in 1981, the favored, top-seeded DePaul Blue Demons were hanging on to a 48–47 lead against the No. 9 seed St. Joseph's Hawks with 13 seconds left when Skip "Money" Dillard went to the foul line with a one-and-one. Dillard, their best free-throw shooter, was given the nickname by his DePaul teammates because his foul shots were like "money in the bank." But at this critical time, his bank account was empty because he missed the first attempt. The Hawks rebounded and scored the winning basket on a layup as time expired.

* * *

Steve Smith had a chance to send his Michigan State Spartans to the Elite Eight in 1990 in the final moments of a Southeast Regional semifinal game against Georgia Tech. With his team winning, 75–73, and only five seconds remaining, Smith was shooting a one-and-one with the opportunity to put the game away. But he missed the front end, and the Yellow Jackets's Kenny Anderson raced down the court and hit a 20-footer as time expired, sending the game into overtime. Georgia Tech went on to win, 81–80.

* * *

In the 1994 East Regional semifinals, the Connecticut Huskies and Florida Gators were tied in the closing seconds. UConn's star Donyell Marshall drove to the basket and was fouled with 3.4 seconds left. Marshall, a 75 percent free-throw shooter and Big East Player of the Year, was the man that the Huskies wanted on the line. He promptly missed both shots, and Florida eventually won, 69–60, in overtime.

* * *

With Mississippi leading, 69–67, with 4.1 seconds remaining in a 1998 Midwest Regional opener, Ansu Sesay, a second-team All-American, stepped to the line for two free throws and a chance to virtually assure a Rebel victory over Valparaiso. But he missed both shots and the rebound bounced off a Mississippi player out of bounds, giving the Crusaders possession with 2.5 seconds remaining. That was just enough time for Drew Bryce to nail a three-pointer at the buzzer for an upset victory.

* * *

In a 2002 South Regional semifinal game, underdog Indiana was up by two points over top-seeded defending champion Duke with 11 seconds left when the Hoosiers' A.J. Moye went to the charity stripe, believing he could seal the upset. He sank both shots to give Indiana a 74–70 lead.

But then the Blue Devils pushed the ball up court and got it to Jason Williams, the Naismith Player of the Year, who drilled a three-pointer as Indiana guard Dane Fife inexplicably committed a foul with four seconds left. The Duke star had a chance for an extraordinary four-point play that would tie the game and send it into overtime. He confidently stepped to the line—and missed.

"Sometimes the ball doesn't bounce your way," he lamented.

"You can call us bad. You can call us thugs. You can call us hoodlums. But at the end of that, please call us national champions too."
—UNLV's Larry Johnson after his team destroyed Duke, 103–73, in 1990 for the title

COACHING QUIRKS

See Ya Later

Wyoming Cowboys coach Everett Shelton was so fed up with his players at halftime of their semifinal game during the 1943 NCAA Tournament that he walked out on them—and didn't return until the final quarter.

The 30-2 Cowboys were playing the 19-6 Texas Longhorns in the Western Regional final in Kansas City. The winner would go on to face Georgetown in New York for the title. Early in the second quarter, Texas jumped out to a 13-point lead, doubling the score against Wyoming, 26–13, which was a considerable deficit back in those days of low-scoring games. However, the Cowboys managed to cut the margin to six, 33–27, by halftime.

"Ev Shelton was our coach and he was a master psychologist," said Wyoming star Kenny Sailors in an interview with the late Denver columnist Dick Conner. "He walked in and never said a word until he finally turned to us and said, 'Well, boys, it looks like this is it. We didn't go all the way like I thought we might. I'll just tell you what. I'll go back to the hotel and start packing things up, and I'll see you toward the end of the game.' And he didn't come back until the end of the third quarter. By then, we had finally gone ahead."

With their coach back on the bench for the final period, the Cowboys knocked off the Longhorns, 58–54.

The following week, Wyoming once again was forced to come from behind. Trailing Georgetown 31–26, with six minutes left in the game, the Cowboys went on a rampage, outscoring the Hoyas, 20–3, the rest of the way to claim the championship. This time, Shelton stayed on the bench the whole game.

All Tied Up

During the 1948 NCAA Tournament, Baylor coach Bill Henderson got himself tied up in knots—literally.

"Mr. Bill," as his players called him, had a nervous habit of tying and untying his shoes at critical points in a game so he wouldn't have to watch a play unfold. He spent a lot of time bent over on the bench.

In the Western Regional in Kansas City, the Bears trailed by 17 points at halftime against the Washington Huskies before storming back to win, 64–62. "Mr. Bill tied the heck out of his shoes in that game," player Bill DeWitt told writer Art Stricklin in *Baylor Magazine*.

Baylor's next opponent was 22-4 Kansas State, considered the favorite. Once again, Baylor trailed by double digits in the first half but rallied for a 60–52 win. According to Stricklin, in the final minutes when the Bears were assured of victory, point guard Jackie Robinson (no, not the baseball player) dribbled past Henderson, who was sitting nervously on the bench, and told him to relax.

The players left immediately after the game, dashing to the station for the train that would take them to New York City for their first (and only) national title bid, against Kentucky's Fabulous Five, who owned a 33-2 record.

Recalling the moments after the Kansas State victory, player Ralph Pulley told Stricklin, "There was no ceremony or anything; we just had to run for the train. I don't even know if there was a trophy or who got it."

Like so many times before, the Bears fell behind in the championship game and trailed the Wildcats at the half, 29–16, as Henderson kept tying and untying his shoes.

Too bad he couldn't tie up Kentucky stars Ralph Beard and Alex Groza. They combined to score 26 points in a 58–42 thrashing of Baylor.

Not that it would have changed the outcome, but the Bears had trouble adjusting to the Madison Square Garden atmosphere. "It seemed like there were nineteen thousand fans and they were all smoking," Robinson told Stricklin. "We could barely see the other end of the court, and at halftime our lungs were hurting with all that smoke."

The Tall and the Short of It
In one of the wackiest attempts to psyche out an opponent, North Carolina Tar Heels coach Frank McGuire tried to toy with the mind of Kansas star Wilt Chamberlain at the start of the 1957 championship game in Kansas City.

At the time, the 7-foot-1 Jayhawk center was the most dominant player in college basketball and was expected to help bring the title back to Kansas. Even though the Tar Heels had a perfect 31-0 record and were ranked No. 1, many oddsmakers considered them the underdogs because they didn't have anyone big enough to challenge Wilt the Stilt.

So the crafty coach conjured up a scheme to rattle the big man at the tip-off. As the players took to the court,

McGuire sent in his smallest player, 5-foot-10 guard Tommy Kearns, to jump center against Chamberlain. On the coach's orders, Kearns squatted all the way down before the jump, making the scene even more ludicrous. The fans laughed and the Tar Heels smirked at the outlandish sight. Chamberlain looked bemused, wondering what other tricks McGuire had up his sleeve.

"I told him [Kearns] if he jumped high enough, he might reach Wilt's stomach," McGuire recalled afterward. "You're not going to get the tap anyway, so why waste a big man? Wilt looked freakish standing there so far above our man."

The coach was always looking for a way to give his team the edge. In fact, he had already displayed his shrewd gamesmanship during warm-ups before the game.

The Jayhawks came onto the floor first and took the bench that the NCAA had assigned them. When the Tar Heels hit the court, their manager brought his equipment over to the Kansas bench, claiming that North Carolina always had the bench closest to its basket in the second half.

In the book *CBS Presents Stories from the Final Four,* edited by Matt Fulks, Kansas assistant coach Jerry Waugh recalled, "Needless to say, [Kansas coach Dick Harp] was madder than hell and talked to tournament director

Reaves Peters, who was also the commissioner of our league. The rules of the tournament were preset and Reaves should have gone to the Carolina manager and told them to move to the other bench. Instead, Reaves said, 'Dick, they're our guests since we're hosting the tournament. Let them have what they want.' So Dick was upset from the outset."

As he did before every game, McGuire waited until the last moment to leave the locker room and walk to the bench so everyone could see him in one of his many snappy, tailor-made suits. This time, however, there was a ruckus near the scorer's table between McGuire and the Kansas fans, who were shouting insults at him. But if McGuire was upset, he didn't show it. In fact, he figured the distraction was to his advantage, considering that virtually every seat in the arena was filled with Jayhawks fans.

McGuire's mind games seemed to work, at least in the opening minutes. The Tar Heels jumped out to an early 19–7 lead and controlled the tempo, slowing it down, and double- and triple-teaming Chamberlain. But, in the second half Wilt brought his team back for a short-lived lead, only to lose in triple overtime, 54–53. He had scored 23 points, but only six on field goals.

DID YOU KNOW . . .

• The 1957 champion Tar Heels could have been called the Big Apples. All the starters were from the New York City area and personally recruited by Frank McGuire, who grew up there and had coached St. John's of New York to the title game against Kansas five years earlier. It was a common joke during McGuire's stint at North Carolina that the New York subway ended in Chapel Hill.

NO SYMPATHY

During an early round game in the 1966 NCAA Tournament, Kentucky Wildcats player Pat Riley was hoping for a little sympathy from Coach Adolph Rupp.

Fat chance.

"I drove hard to the basket, missed the shot, got the rebound, missed again and again and again," recalled Riley, who went on to coach the Los Angeles Lakers and Miami Heat. "I got creamed on the final rebound but no foul was called and I was knocked to the floor and slid right in front of Coach Rupp. I was lying on the floor exhausted, hoping for a little compassion from him. He looked down at me, looked out on the floor and then said, 'Pat, get your ass up! There goes your man with the ball!'"

Coaching Bombshells

No Final Four team was more shocked after winning a
semifinal game than the 1975 UCLA Bruins. They weren't
surprised they had edged Louisville, 75–74, in overtime.
What stunned them was what happened in the locker
room afterward.

Their mentor, John Wooden—the Wizard of
Westwood, a coaching legend who up to that point had
guided UCLA to six consecutive titles—blindsided them
by announcing he was retiring.

"We came running into the locker room and were very
noisy," forward Wilbert Olinde recalled days later in the
school paper, the *Daily Bruin*. "Coach came into the room
and asked us all to be quiet. He told us he was proud of
the way we came back from being down. He said that winning wasn't everything, but he really wanted this win,
because he is bowing out. After that we were all quiet. He
said a few more things and then left the room."

The timing of the stunning announcement surprised
even Wooden himself. He told Cal Fussman of *UCLA
Magazine*, "Coming off the floor after the NCAA semifinal win over Louisville, it just hit me. Time to go. It was
an emotional thing. I can't explain it. I went to the dress-
ing room and congratulated my players on a fine game. I
said, 'I don't know how we'll do Monday night against

Kentucky, but I think we'll do all right. Regardless of the outcome of the game, I never had a team give me more pleasure. I'm very proud of you. This will be the last team I'll ever coach.'

"They were shocked. I went to the press and told them, and my athletic director almost fainted. My wife didn't know. I didn't know myself until it happened."

Athletic director J.D. Morgan spent half the night trying to talk Wooden out of retiring. The 64-year-old coach acknowledged he was concerned about the health of his wife, Nell. She did not try to talk him out of retirement.

Wooden said his only regret was the announcement overshadowed what he called a close-to-perfect game by UCLA and Louisville. Two nights later, UCLA faced Kentucky for the championship. Even though Wooden stressed that his players try to win the title for themselves, they were determined to give him a going away present. And they did, whipping Kentucky, 92–85, to hand Wooden his 10th NCAA championship.

In 27 years with the Bruins, Wooden finished with a 620-147 record. In his final 12 seasons, his teams achieved an incredible 335-22 mark.

* * *

John Wooden wasn't the only championship coach to drop a bombshell on his team. Al McGuire did it to his Marquette Warriors halfway through the 1976–77 season. His decision to retire at the end of the year staggered his players, but it gave them an incentive to make him go out a winner.

When McGuire announced he was giving up coaching, "it was a shock to everyone," guard Butch Lee told Jeff D'Alessio of *The Sporting News*. "We were in a restaurant in downtown Milwaukee. I think it was after class. We were waiting for him to show up and we saw our trainer come in and he was crying. We didn't know what to expect. We knew it was something serious, but we didn't know what. We had such great teams there. No one ever expected Al was going to leave the team. It was a shock. It all happened so fast."

When a friend asked why he was giving up coaching, McGuire cracked, "I'm tired of telling seventeen-year-olds I can't live without them."

The team didn't respond very well to the news. "After that, we lost three in a row," said Lee. "It affected us pretty hard."

But the street-smart, wise-cracking, hot-tempered coach got his team back on track and they struggled their way to the championship game with one thought in mind—win it for their coach. The Warriors then beat North Carolina, 67–59, at the Omni in Atlanta.

In the final seconds, McGuire burst into tears when the realization struck him that Marquette was about to win the national title in his final game as a coach. He had paid his dues—mentoring youngsters in Catholic Youth Organization Leagues and Police Athletic Leagues, driving players to games at Belmont Abbey, baby-sitting freshmen players at Dartmouth, scouring the seamy back alleys and cracked outdoor courts of his hometown New York City for talent. And now this. A national championship.

Breaking away from a hug from his longtime assistant coach, Hank Raymonds, McGuire hurried off from the impending on-court celebration for the privacy of the Marquette locker room, where he unleashed his emotions. Holding a towel to his eyes, he sobbed while pacing back and forth. When he regained his composure, he returned to the arena for the ceremonies while Marquette fans chanted, "Al's last hurrah! Al's last hurrah!"

Later, when asked by reporters why he didn't join in the celebration right after the buzzer, he replied, "I'm not ashamed to cry. It's just that I don't like to do it in front of people."

Twenty years of college coaching and it came down to the final game before he won it all. "Normally," he said, "street fighters like me don't end up in lace."

DID YOU KNOW . . .

• The official *NCAA Men's Final Four Records Book* includes a team photo of each year's champion going back to 1939. All except one picture show the same standard poses of guys in their uniforms either sitting on a bench or standing in a semi-circle with their arms at their sides. For their official photo, the Marquette players wore flashy, different-colored tuxedoes—some were even in tails—and posed around a vintage Rolls-Royce convertible.

"Coaching college is not pizza parties and getting the team together at the A&W stand. People can't understand my players screaming back at me, but it's healthy. Also, I notice that the screaming always comes when we're fifteen, twenty points ahead. When it's tied, they're all listening very carefully to what I have to say."
—Marquette Coach Al McGuire

Can It, Bobby

Indiana coach Bobby Knight—no stranger to controversy—grabbed the headlines from his team shortly after the Hoosiers squashed Louisiana State, 67–49, in the 1981 semifinals.

He shoved a loudmouth LSU fan into a garbage can, according to witnesses. Knight said he and some friends headed for dinner in the Hoosiers's hotel in Cherry Hill, New Jersey. As they walked through the restaurant bar, one of the 200 LSU fans who were staying at that same hotel told Knight, "Congratulations."

The coach had been annoyed with the Tiger boosters earlier that morning because whenever his players walked between the team's meeting room and the breakfast room, LSU fans hollered, "Tiger bait! Tiger bait!"

So when he heard the fan offer congratulations, Knight wasn't very receptive.

"As I walked past this guy," the coach explained at a press conference the next day, "I turned to him and said over my shoulder, 'Well, we really weren't Tiger bait after all, were we?' And I kept on walking with the people in my party."

Knight said the fan—Louis Bonnecaze Jr., an accountant from Baton Rouge—shouted an obscenity at him, then repeated it. Recalled Knight, "I walked over—I did a little more than walk over, I walked swiftly over—and I said, 'Would you like to say again what you just said?'

"He said, 'I gave you a compliment and you were very

sarcastic and rude to me.'

"I said, 'No, I wasn't sarcastic and rude to you. I just threw something back at you that our kids have been hearing all day long.' He said, 'Well, you're still an asshole.' I grabbed him, shoved him up against the wall and turned and walked away."

News accounts said Bonnecaze wound up in a garbage can.

"We didn't trade shoves," Knight told the press. "I did all the shoving. And we didn't trade insults. He did all the insulting."

Bonnecaze called police, but no charges were filed.

Knight said he frequently had been called names in arenas but learned to put up with it. "I probably ignore ten thousand things for every one that I get upset about," he said at the time. "But I'll be damned if I'll take that in a public place. If it happens again tomorrow, I'll do exactly the same thing."

At the end of the press conference when Knight took questions, a sportswriter asked, "Did the fan go cleanly into the garbage can, or did he rim out?"

Bench Brouhaha

During UCLA's game against Kansas in the 1971 semifinal, there was more tension on the sidelines than in the game itself.

Bruins head coach John Wooden and assistant coach Denny Crum got into a heated argument. Early in the game, Crum told guard Terry Schofield to go in for Kenny Booker. Wooden ordered Schofield to sit down and threatened to kick Crum to the end of the bench. Later in the contest, Wooden and Crum got into another testy quarrel over strategy, causing the head coach to thunder, "I'm the coach of this team, and don't tell me how to coach my team!"

UCLA guard Henry Bibby had to step in and act as peacemaker. UCLA went on to win the game and then the championship. Crum moved on to take the head coaching job at Louisville.

And wouldn't you know, he wound up facing his mentor the following year when Louisville met UCLA in the 1972 semifinals. Crum apparently had a lot to learn from the master because the Bruins smashed the Cardinals, 96–77.

Driven by Superstition

As a college coach, Larry Brown was superstitious and looked for luck anywhere he could find it, whether it was from a penny or from a person.

At the start of the 1988 NCAA Tournament, the

Kansas Jayhawks weren't given much of a chance to win the title, not with a 21-11 record. "Not in my wildest dreams," said Brown, who began the tournament by packing extra clothes so he could go recruiting as soon as his team lost. But they surprised most everyone—including their coach—when they defeated the Kansas State Wildcats, 71–58, in the Midwest Regional in Pontiac, Michigan, to earn a spot in the Final Four.

Brown had found his lucky charm.

In an interview with Gary Bedore, the *Lawrence* (Kansas) *Journal-World* assistant sports editor, Kansas' athletic director Bob Frederick recalled, "I went in the locker room after we beat K-State. Larry came up to me and said, 'I need a favor from you.' I said, 'No problem,' without even knowing what it was. I started to think, 'My gosh, what's he gonna ask for?'

"Larry said, 'I want to bring Jimmy the bus driver back to Kansas City with us.' I said, 'That's great, Coach. No problem.' "

Greyhound driver Jimmy Dunlop had chauffeured the team to and from the airport and hotel during the Jayhawks's stay in the Detroit area for the Regionals, where they had beaten Vanderbilt and Kansas State. What Brown wanted now was to have Dunlop drive the team bus in Kansas City, site of the Final Four.

"Bringing Jimmy to Kansas City was fairly important to him," Frederick said.

"We got some criticism [for] spending taxpayers's money bringing a bus driver back home with us. Of course, the taxpayers didn't pay for Jimmy. Greyhound got so much publicity out of it they paid for him and sent us all [miniature] Greyhound buses."

If anyone scoffed at Brown's superstition, they backed off when Kansas won the championship in an 83–79 triumph over favored Oklahoma—a team that had previously beaten KU twice in the regular season.

Dunlop was considered such a good omen that he participated in the Jayhawks's victory parade down Massachusetts Street. He waved to the crowds from the back seat of a convertible, signed autographs and posed with fans for pictures.

In 2002, Brown's successor, Roy Williams, figured that if the superstition worked for Brown it would work for him. So when Kansas went to the Final Four in Atlanta, Williams asked that bus driver Bruce Guffey, of Lawrence, Kansas, chauffeur the team. Guffey had been behind the wheel for the Jayhawks at Midwest Regional ports of call in St. Louis and Madison, Wisconsin.

Guffey, of Arrow Stage Lines, drove an empty eight-wheel, 50-passenger cruiser 13 hours over two days from

Lawrence to Atlanta to meet the team. Unfortunately, what worked for Brown didn't work for Williams. Kansas fell to eventual champion Maryland in the semifinals, 97–88.

DID YOU KNOW . . .
• The 11 losses suffered by Kansas in 1988 were the most by a champion in NCAA history.

The Winless Coach Who Won

Steve Fisher coached the Michigan Wolverines to the 1989 NCAA championship even though he had never won a regular-season game.

But then, he had never lost one, either. That's because he became the first interim coach in Division I hoops history to win a national title.

Just two days before the start of post-season tournament action, Michigan's regular head coach, Bill Frieder, announced that he had accepted a job to run the Arizona State basketball program. Frieder expected to leave Michigan after he coached the Wolverines in the NCAA Tournament. However, Athletic Director Bo Schembechler, angered by Frieder's defection, fired the coach.

Then Schembechler appointed Fisher, who was Frieder's assistant coach, to run the team. It was the first time the career assistant had been a head coach since he was a high school teacher.

Doomsayers predicted that the traumatic, last-minute upheaval caused by the coaching change would so demoralize the 24-7 Wolverines that they likely would collapse in the early rounds.

In the opener of the Southeast Regional in Atlanta, No. 3 seed Michigan struggled against No. 14 seed Xavier of Ohio, but won, 92–87. "I was scared to death prior to walking from the locker room onto the floor," Fisher confessed to reporters. "But after the ball was thrown up, I think I settled into a routine that was business as usual."

Next, Michigan beat South Alabama and then North Carolina—a team that had eliminated the Wolverines in the tourney the previous two years. Reaching the Elite Eight, Fisher told reporters, "I'm just going to hang on for the ride as long as I can."

After crushing Virginia, the Wolverines, who were averaging 92 points per game, arrived in Seattle for the Final Four. In the semis, they edged Illinois, 83–81, on a last-second shot in a game that featured 33 lead changes. "If this is a dream, don't wake me up until Tuesday morning," said Fisher.

Throughout the tournament, Fisher had to deal with people who confused him with Frieder. A CBS announcer referred to him as "Steve Frieder" during a post-game interview and even a Michigan sports publicist called him by his predecessor's name.

But all that changed when Fisher's Wolverines—who were given little chance of advancing beyond the first round without Frieder—won the NCAA title in an 80–79 overtime thriller over Seton Hall.

"Maybe I ought to retire right now," Fisher joked after the game.

A few days later, before the Wolverines made the traditional White House visit to show off their championship trophy, Schembechler took the "interim" off Fisher's title and appointed him head coach.

"Life's crazy," Fisher said at the time. "And I'm happy to be along for the ride."

Temper, Temper

Marquette coach Al McGuire admitted that his temper probably cost his team the 1974 championship.

The Warriors were beating the North Carolina State Wolfpack, 28–27, late in the first half when McGuire was hit with two technical fouls for arguing a little too vociferously with the refs. David Thompson converted the technical foul shots and the momentum shifted. The Wolfpack scored ten unanswered points in a 53-second span to turn Marquette's one-point advantage into a 37–28 deficit. The Warriors trudged to the locker room at halftime trailing, 39–30. They never recovered and lost, 76–64.

Marquette star Maurice Lucas was furious afterward at McGuire, and in the locker room, he shouted, "Thanks for losing the game for us, Coach!"

McGuire fired back, "That makes up for all the games I won for you!"

After he cooled down, Lucas told reporters, "We never got back on our feet after that" spate of technicals. Even N.C. State's David Thompson agreed. "The technicals sure gave us a lift," he said.

To his credit, McGuire took the blame, telling the press, "I cost us the game."

T-Totaler

North Carolina's Dean Smith—the coach with the most victories in college basketball—suffered his most mortifying exit from a tournament in a defeat to his former assistant.

Losing to Roy Williams's Kansas Jayhawks in the 1991 semifinals was bad enough for the veteran Tar Heel coach.

But even worse, Smith was forced to leave the court in humiliation, ejected by the referees after being slapped with his second technical foul.

One of the story lines of the Final Four matchup between the 26-7 Jayhawks and the 29-5 Tar Heels at the Hoosier Dome was the shared history of the two head coaches. Williams had been Smith's assistant coach at North Carolina for ten years before moving in 1988 to Kansas—the school where Smith was a member of its 1952 championship team.

The Jayhawks staked out a 10-point lead in the second half and then watched it disappear during a Tar Heel rally. But Kansas prevailed down the stretch and won, 79–73. Smith wasn't around to see the end because he had been given the boot after his second technical foul.

Smith received the first technical with 2:58 left in the first half for complaining over a foul called against center Pete Chilcutt. According to the players on the bench, Smith's beef wasn't anything that warranted even a warning. They said he yelled to the refs, "They're pushing us, too! They're pushing us, too!"

Williams said after the game that Smith did not deserve the first T. "I heard what he said," Williams told reporters. "I don't think he was saying enough to get that technical."

The second technical came after North Carolina forward Rick Fox fouled out with 35 seconds remaining in the game. Smith said later he left the coaching box to walk a substitute to the scorer's table and buy time for his team. The coaching box is a designated area along the sideline that coaches are not supposed to leave except to break up a fight or to seek information from the scorer or timer during a time-out or intermission. The penalty for leaving the box otherwise is a technical foul.

But Smith contended that since Fox had fouled out, it was a dead-ball situation, so he was entitled to leave the box. However, referee Pete Pavia pointed out that the rules are clear: A coach can't go out of the box, even in a dead-ball situation.

So Smith had to leave the court following just his third ejection of a coaching career that began way back in 1955. "It was kind of embarrassing," Smith admitted, "especially being a Kansas alumnus."

But rather than fume and rant, Smith went out with class. After being ordered to leave, Smith walked over to the Kansas bench, where he shook hands and exchanged warm words with Williams. He then shook hands with virtually every player on the Jayhawk bench before departing.

Recalled Williams, "He said he didn't mean for it to end that way and that we had played very well and that he was happy for us."

Righting a Wrong

Dean Smith has set the record straight: Although the official box score for the 1952 championship game at the time did not list his name, he did play. For all of 27 seconds.

Long before he became a coaching icon, Smith was a seldom-used reserve player on the Kansas Jayhawks throughout the 1951–52 season. He made a brief appearance in their 80–63 triumph over St. John's for the national title. For decades it irked Smith that his name was not in the official box score.

Knowing he had played, Smith, who by now was a North Carolina coaching legend, studied game films and determined he had racked up a whopping 27 seconds of playing time in the big game. Okay, so it was less time than some players take at the free-throw line, but at least he got in. Armed with the proof, friends successfully lobbied the NCAA to correct the error nearly 40 years after the fact.

"That may not seem important to some people, but I was so proud to be a part of that team that I wanted it recorded I played in a championship game," Smith told sportswriter Bill Mayer of the *Lawrence* (Kansas) *Journal-World*. "I was greatly relieved when it got corrected.

There's a lot more to this game than fame or money.
There's the tremendous pride you have in being with the
kinds of people I associated with at KU. No amount of
money can provide that."

It's a Small World

For Kentucky coach Rick Pitino, winning the 1996 championship meant beating both his close friend and his
former mentor in the Final Four.

In the semifinals at East Rutherford, New Jersey, the
Wildcats faced off against the Massachusetts Minutemen,
who were coached by Pitino's good friend, John Calipari.
Eight years earlier, Pitino, a UMass alumnus, was on a
search committee looking for a new basketball coach for
his alma mater. It was Pitino's recommendation that
helped Calipari get the job.

Earlier in the 1995–96 season, Kentucky, which was
ranked No. 1 at the time, was upset by UMass, 92–82. "If
we win that game, we don't win the national championship," Pitino told reporters after the season. He felt that
the loss "taught us more about our team than any win on
our schedule."

The Wildcats were ready the next time the teams met
in the semifinals and overpowered Massachusetts, 81–74.
Then, when Syracuse beat Mississippi State in the other

semifinal, 77–69, Pitino had to match wits with the man who taught him much about coaching.

Back in 1976, when Pitino was an assistant coach at the University of Hawaii, he got married. While on his honeymoon in New York, he received a call from Syracuse coach Jim Boeheim, who said he was considering Pitino for a position as his assistant.

The offer to interview came on Pitino's wedding night. Boeheim insisted on discussing the job with him minutes after Pitino had carried his wife across the threshold of a New York hotel. So Pitino interrupted his honeymoon to interview for the job, which he got. He served two seasons under Boeheim before landing his first head coaching job in 1978 with Boston University.

Fast forward to 1996. Now Pitino's Wildcats were going up against his one-time mentor's Orangemen for the national championship. Boeheim had already beaten Pitino in a Final Four game in 1987 when Pitino coached Providence, which lost to Syracuse, 77–63.

But in 1996, Pitino got even as Kentucky stomped Syracuse, 76–67, to capture the crown.

*"I am immensely proud of you. You're really the best. You've
proved it. Now don't let it change you. You are champions and you
must act like champions. You met some people going up to the top.
You will meet the same people going down."*
—UCLA coach John Wooden, to his players after they capped a perfect
30-0 season by beating Duke, 98–83, for the 1964 national title

HEART AND SPIRIT, GUTS AND TEARS

Head Strong

David Thompson, one of the greatest college basketball players of all time, heard plenty of cheers during his playing days. But nothing was as loud as the roaring ovation he received during a playoff game just for showing up—just for being alive.

Possessing whip-quick moves, kangaroo-like leaping abilities, and a laser shooting touch, the 6-foot-4 junior forward with the big Afro dominated both ends of the court. Dubbed "the Skywalker" because of his 44-inch vertical leap, Thompson reportedly was able to pluck a quarter off the top of the backboard.

In 1974, when he was named AP's National Player of

the Year, the North Carolina State star led the Wolfpack in what many consider the greatest game in Atlantic Coast Conference history—a heart-pounding 103–100 overtime tingler against Maryland for the right to represent the league in the NCAA Tournament (before there were at-large bids).

The Pack, ranked No. 1 in the nation, entered the tourney with a 26-1 record, its lone blemish an embarrassing 84–66 defeat to UCLA, which was at the top of the rankings then, but was now No. 2. Pundits figured N.C. State had the best shot at dethroning the Bruins, winners of an unprecedented seven straight championships.

After dispatching Providence, 92–78, N.C. State took on the Pittsburgh Panthers on its home court in Reynolds Coliseum in Raleigh. Midway through the first half, after the Panthers had built an unexpected 12-point lead, Thompson soared through the lane and swatted away a Pittsburgh shot, but he was whistled for goaltending and the basket counted.

The call paled in comparison to what else happened on the play. At the top of his leap, the toe of Thompson's shoe caught teammate Phil Spence's shoulder. Thompson cartwheeled in the air and his head slammed onto the wood floor with a sickening thud. (Replays showed that his head was perpendicular to his body when he landed.)

Fans and teammates gasped, fearing he was paralyzed or dead, and a pall settled over the arena. Wrote sportswriter Tim Peeler at gopack.com, "C.A. Dillon, the long-time public address announcer who attended almost every game ever played at Reynolds, doesn't remember a moment that was ever so eerily quiet as when Thompson lay on the floor getting frantic medical attention."

Thompson was unconscious, lying in a puddle of blood, and didn't move for four minutes. He didn't wake up until 10 minutes later when he was being wheeled into an ambulance.

"That was pretty scary," Thompson recalled years later in *Basketball Digest*. "The whole team didn't know if I was going to make it or not. I didn't move for a long time. There was blood everywhere. It looked like it was coming out of my ear, but actually it was coming from the back of my head."

He was rushed to Rex Hospital for X-rays. The injury looked so bad at first that a hospital staffer stayed on the phone with a producer for CBS in case Walter Cronkite had to break into regular programming for a news bulletin saying that the nation's best player had died.

Thankfully, the diagnosis was not nearly as grim as feared. Thompson had suffered a severe concussion and needed 15 stitches to sew up the gash in his head. He was woozy and in pain, but, at his insistence, doctors agreed to release him from the hospital.

Meanwhile, the Wolfpack—not knowing their team-mate's condition—didn't get rattled by his injury. In fact, the players seemed inspired and determined to win for their fallen star, and so they battled back to take the lead at halftime. Minutes later, Dillon, the public address announcer, received a phone call from the hospital. Dillon quieted the crowd by starting this announcement: "We have a report from the hospital." Silence. "Doctors say that David Thompson is going to be fine."

Wrote Peeler, "The place erupted, the loudest cheer Reynolds had ever heard. Until a few minutes later. [Wolfpack player Tom] Burleson was getting ready to shoot free throws when he saw Thompson, his head band-aged from chin to scalp, come in the door. He dropped the ball and raced over to his friend, eager to welcome him back, but scared to hug him. The rest of the team fol-lowed.

"Then [Coach Norm] Sloan and the rest of the sell-out crowd saw Thompson back in the arena. 'There was never a louder moment in the history of Reynolds Coliseum,' Dillon said. 'To me, that was the most memorable moment ever.'"

In recalling the scare, Thompson said, "What I told all

the guys is my Afro saved me. The Afro acted like padding. I came back into the arena with a turban-like bandage on my head. I got a great ovation from the crowd. It was a touching moment."

As Thompson sat on the bench and groggily watched, his relieved teammates hammered Pittsburgh, 100–72.

Next up: UCLA. Everyone wondered if Thompson could play. But he figured as long as he could see one basket and not two when he shot during practice, he would definitely be in the starting lineup in the Final Four clash in Greensboro, North Carolina, against the dreaded Bruins.

Sporting a 15-stitch memento in the back of his head, Thompson willed his team to victory, scoring 28 points and grabbing 10 rebounds. Throughout the game, UCLA would burst ahead, only to have the Wolfpack catch up. In the second half, N.C. State was down by 11, yet stormed back to force overtime, and then another one.

In the second OT, the Wolfpack trailed by seven, but once again they refused to give up. Thompson hit a basket to cut the lead to four, later drained a 12-footer with 53 seconds remaining to give his team the lead, and made two game-clinching free throws in the final seconds. N.C. State won, 80–77, ending UCLA's seven-year reign as national champions and its 38-game playoff winning streak.

In the anticlimactic championship game, the Wolfpack downed Marquette, 76–64. Thompson, who had 21 points and seven rebounds, was named the tournament's Most Outstanding Player. Not bad for a hard-headed player.

"People have to be given the freedom to show the heart they possess. I think it's a leader's responsibility to provide that type of freedom."
—Duke coach Mike Krzyzewski

Giving It Your All

When you play in the NCAA Tournament, you leave it all on the court. Indiana State's Kelyn Block certainly did—with his blood, sweat, and three broken teeth. He lost them in a nasty collision, but you should have seen the other guy. Despite the seriousness of their injuries, both played on in heroic efforts.

In the opening round of the 2001 South Regional at the Pyramid in Memphis, the No. 13 seed Indiana State Sycamores were working on an upset of the No. 4 seed Oklahoma Sooners, who were ranked 13th in the nation. With ISU nursing a 59–57 lead in the final minute, Block, a 6-foot-2, 200-pound guard, fouled Sooners guard Hollis Price, who was driving down the lane. As both players fell to the floor, Price's right elbow accidentally smashed into Block's mouth with such ferocity that Price's triceps tendon was slashed while three of Block's lower front teeth were shattered and went flying near the baseline.

Block stood for a moment and then fell to the floor, bleeding and in pain. He was quickly ushered to the locker room, and his teammates thought he was done for the night.

Meanwhile, Price's elbow was bleeding so badly from the severe laceration that the sophomore had to be replaced at the free-throw line while the trainer attended to the injury.

"Hollis had his triceps tendon torn," Oklahoma coach Kelvin Sampson said later. "He was really gouged right down to the triceps muscle. I didn't think there was any way he could have stayed on the floor."

After his arm was bandaged up, the plucky Price went back into the game with his team trailing, 61–59. Even though his elbow was on the brink of going numb, Price took an inbounds pass, raced up court and banked in a tying shot with 18 seconds left to force overtime.

About a minute after the extra period began, Block sprinted out of the tunnel and back to the Sycamores bench to the cheers of amazed ISU fans. Block, who had been cleaned up and given a strong dose of Tylenol in the locker room, was wearing a mouthpiece to protect his swollen mouth. He had no intention of acting as a cheerleader. He was going to play.

"When he ran back out on the court right at the beginning of overtime, that was sort of a relief," Sycamores coach Royce Waltman said.

The moment Block entered the game, he promptly stole an Oklahoma pass and drove in for a layup that put his team ahead for good. The courageous junior scored five of ISU's nine points in OT and led the Sycamores to a stirring 70–68 victory.

Seeing Block return to the game "was a huge lift," teammate Matt Renn said afterwards. "I don't know if we could have done it without him. He's in a lot of pain. He's a tough kid."

Block, unable to speak to the media, was whisked to the University of Memphis Hospital's dental office, where the next day he had three root canals and his broken teeth capped.

"I'm sure if anybody else on any team got hit like that, they'd want to go back in," he told Mark Bennett of the Terre Haute (Indiana) *Tribune-Star*. He said he has few lasting effects from the collision. "When it's cold outside, I can feel they're not real. But other than that, I'm fine."

Price got the worst of the impact. His wound was so

serious that he needed three surgeries on his right elbow. Doctors told him that he came perilously close to having his arm amputated. "The tendon pulled away from my elbow and it just missed my nerve, which would have cost me the arm," Price said.

But some good came out of the freakish injury. Price was able to develop his offhand skills. "My right arm was immobilized for two months, so I could only shoot and dribble with my left hand," he explained. "That ended up paying off a whole lot." Under his leadership and scoring the next year, the Sooners made it to the Final Four.

In a classic understatement, Coach Sampson said, "Kelyn and Hollis, both those kids play so doggone hard."

A Shot in the Hip

Nothing was going to stop Sam Aubrey from playing basketball—not even a crippling bullet wound.

Aubrey was a 6-foot-4 forward for the Oklahoma A&M Aggies (now the oklahoma state cowboys) in 1943 when he left school to join the service. In September 1944, he was in the middle of a firefight in Italy when he was shot in the hip. The injury was so severe that he spent nearly a year in the hospital. The prognosis wasn't good. The doctor said Aubrey would need a cane and that by the time he was 35, he would be confined in a wheelchair.

Aubrey refused to believe it. In the fall of 1945, he returned to the campus in Stillwater, which displayed the championship banner it had won earlier that year. Even though he was limping on a cane, he told Coach Hank Iba that he would play again because he wanted to defend the title.

"The poor guy," Iba recalled in an interview with long-time sports columnist Bob Hurt of *The Daily Oklahoman*. "He couldn't make it the length of the court at first." But Aubrey practiced hard and worked out endlessly until "he ended up starting every damn ballgame. He was a team player—not a lot of flash—but he did his job."

Aubrey was one of four players on the 1945–46 squad who had seen action in World War II. Their grittiness and determination—along with player-of-the-year Bob Kurland—were instrumental in bringing the school its second straight NCAA championship.

For You, Hank

The Loyola Marymount Lions played the 1990 tournament with a heavy heart. Their star, Hank Gathers, had collapsed on the court and died just two weeks before the tourney got underway.

His shocking death numbed his teammates, but they regrouped and played their guts out, making a stirring run to the Elite Eight even though they were an 11th seed. And throughout the tourney, Gathers's best friend and teammate, Bo Kimble, made one of the most touching gestures in NCAA history.

Kimble and Gathers grew up together in Philadelphia and led Dobbins Technical High School to the Public League City championship in 1985. The two players were then recruited by Stan Morrison, coach at the University of Southern California. But after Morrison was fired in 1986, Kimble and Gathers transferred to Loyola Marymount, the tiny Los Angeles–area Catholic school that had a team headed by Paul Westhead, former coach of the Los Angeles Lakers.

After sitting out the 1986–87 season as required under NCAA rules for transfer students, the pair ignited LMU's explosive, exciting team. The Lions played a tenacious full-court press and typically took shots within 10 seconds of gaining possession. It was no wonder they were by far the highest-scoring team the nation had ever seen, setting the all-time NCAA Division I record by averaging 122.4 points per game.

"The Hank and Bo Show" captivated college basketball fans. Gathers had led the nation in scoring and rebounding in his junior season by averaging 33 points and 13 rebounds a game. The following year, Kimble averaged

35.3 points a game, tops in the land. So the little school with the big-time players was looking forward to making a name for itself by earning a berth in the NCAA Tournament.

However, there was a serious problem. In early December 1989, Gathers was diagnosed with an abnormal heartbeat after he collapsed during a game. He began taking a prescribed beta blocker that evened his heart rhythm, but he felt it adversely affected his game, so he cut back on the dosage.

On March 4, 1990, LMU was playing Portland for the West Coast Conference championship and an automatic berth to the Big Dance. Midway through the first half with the Lions up, 25–13, Gathers, who had scored eight quick points, slumped to the floor unconscious. Despite frantic resuscitation efforts on the court and a fast response time by emergency technicians, Hank Gathers died.

The game was suspended, and LMU was given the league's automatic bid to the NCAA Tournament, but as a lowly 11th seed. Although hurting from the loss of Gathers, the 23-5 Lions decided to turn their heartache into a positive force—by trying to win for their deceased teammate.

In the opener, LMU smacked No. 6 seed New Mexico State, 111–92, and then crushed defending champion

Michigan, 149–115, while racking up the most points in tournament history. Next, the Lions squeaked past Alabama, 62–60, to make it to the Elite Eight. In reporting LMU's heartrending march through the tournament, *Sports Illustrated* came out with a cover that said, "For You, Hank."

But raw emotion could carry the Lions only so far. They put up a good fight but were knocked out, 131–101, by UNLV, which tallied the second-highest point total in tourney history and went on to win the title.

What many fans remember most about LMU's run was Bo Kimble's tribute at the foul line to his best bud. Bo shot his first free throw of each tournament game left-handed. It was his way to honor Gathers, who was right-handed but struggled so much with his free throws that he began shooting them left-handed. In all four tournament games, Kimble swished his left-handed free throws. "For You, Hank."

Playing for Others

Teams don't reach the Final Four without a lot of talent and heart. But sometimes they get an added boost from an inspired source.

Before the 1980 championship contest, Louisville's Darrell Griffith appeared on tape in the network broadcast to dedicate the game to his lifelong friend, Jerry Stringer, who was dying of cancer. Stringer had been a schoolmate of Griffith and Louisville teammate Bobby Turner when the trio attended Male High School in Louisville. The Cardinals dedicated the 1979–80 season to Stringer.

The day after they won the title, several Louisville players went to Stringer's home to visit their stricken friend. As he lay in bed, the players draped strands of the net around his head. He died a short time later.

* * *

The UNLV Running Rebels said they wanted to win the 1990 title for their "honorary coach," Valerie Pida. Battling cancer since the age of 13, Pida was a UNLV student from 1985 through 1991. During that time she majored in marketing and hotel administration and was a cheerleader, homecoming queen, and Delta Zeta sorority member. In 1987, she received a bone marrow transplant, yet, during her recovery, still managed to cheer for her team from courtside during UNLV's Final Four appearance. She was also cheering when the Rebels won the 1990 championship.

Pida gained national recognition and won hearts with her determination to fight her disease. In 1988 she was named an Unsung American Hero by *Newsweek* magazine.

She died in 1992 at the age of 25 after a valiant 12-year battle with cancer.

* * *

On their way to winning the 1999 championship, every Connecticut Huskies player kept a picture of Joe McGinn in his locker during the tournament.

McGinn, who had been the popular team manager from 1992 through 1995, suffered from kidney disease and died of a heart attack at the age of 26 as the Huskies were preparing for their opening round game in Denver.

It was a tough way to start the tournament, especially for Coach Jim Calhoun. He had become such a close friend to McGinn that the year before, when doctors determined that the young man's legs had to be amputated, it was the coach who broke the news to him. "It was the most emotional thing I've ever done," Calhoun told *Sports Illustrated*. "Much more emotional than a Final Four."

When the Huskies captured the title—becoming the first team since Texas Western in 1966 to win it all on its first trip to the Final Four—Calhoun honored his former manager in a touching way. During the cutting of the net,

Calhoun snipped the final strand and put it back on the rim for McGinn.

* * *

For UConn's Richard Hamilton, who was the game's high scorer with 27 points, inspiration came from his paternal grandfather, Edward, who had died the previous summer after a long battle with lung cancer. Before the game, Hamilton's father, Richard, told the player, "Grandpa wants a national championship." Hamilton, who said he was thinking of his grandfather throughout the game, wore a tattoo on his upper right arm. It was a cross with the inscription EDWARD HAMILTON, OCT. 9, 1922-SEPT. 25, 1998.

During the 2006 tourney, Bucknell players scrawled names or initials on their socks to memorialize two children close to the program.

Tylor Pfeiffer, an 11-year-old ball boy for the team, was killed in a fire two weeks before the tournament started. A week later, assistant coach Brian Goodman's eight-week-old daughter, Sophia, died of complications from a premature birth.

"It really puts into perspective that we're really just playing a game and there are bigger things out there," said

With excitement at a fever pitch, the official game ball is ready for the opening tip-off of the 2006 national championship clash between Florida and UCLA.

CCNY coach Nat Holman waves triumphantly after his Beavers' historic wins over Bradley for the 1950 NCAA title and earlier for the NIT title.

Weary but jubilant North Carolina players hoist coach Frank McGuire on their shoulders, after nipping Kansas 54–53 in triple overtime for the 1957 championship.

Kentucky's Jamaal Magloire blocks the shot of Utah's Britton Johnsen as the Wildcats storm back from a double-digit deficit for the third straight game and win the 1998 title, 78–69.

Illinois' Dee Brown leaps for joy after an amazing Elite Eight comeback when his Illini erased a 15-point deficit in the final four minutes to steal an epic 90–89 victory over Arizona in 2005.

Michigan's Jalen Rose (left) fires up teammate Chris Webber during the 1993 title game with North Carolina. Too bad Rose didn't remind Webber later how many timeouts they had left.

Prairie View's only game in a NCAA Tournament turns into an inglorious affair—the second-worst defeat ever in the event's history. Kansas creams the Panthers, 110–52, in a 1998 opener.

Who can forget Danny Ainge's incredible last-second coast-to-coast dash through all five Notre Dame defenders to score the winning basket in BYU's dramatic 51–50 victory in a 1981 regional.

Duke's Christian Laettner, who had just caught a perfectly thrown 75-foot pass from Grant Hill, shoots the buzzer-beater in a heart-stopping 104–103 overtime thriller against Kentucky in a 1992 regional final.

Valparaiso's Bryce Drew, on the receiving end of a touch-pass from Bill Jenkins, who had caught a lengthy pass from Jamie Sykes, launches a game winning three-pointer at the buzzer to clip Mississippi, 70–69, in a 1998 regional. Below, Bryce is hugged by his dad, coach Homer Drew, for making what is known in Valpo-land as "The Shot."

John Wooden celebrates his 10th and final championship by wearing the cut-down net after UCLA whipped Kentucky, 92–85, in 1975. The win was a going away present from his players who were shocked days earlier when he announced he was retiring.

Top:
Santa Clara's Mark Schmitz (20) and Steve Nash (11) jump for joy after their 15th seeded team—described by one wag as "a motley jumble of eggheads, surfers, and imports"—upset No. 2 seed Arizona, 64–61, in a 1993 opener.

Top Left:
With his head wrapped in bandages and tears streaming down his face, North Carolina State's David Thompson is surrounded by teammates after he returned from the hospital with 15 stitches following a scary fall earlier in the 1974 regional game.

Bottom Left:
Bucknell's Donald Brown celebrates by popping his collar after his 14th seeded team shocked No. 3 seed Kansas, 64–63, in a 2005 opener.

Willie Cager drives the lane in the 1966 title game between Texas Western's all-black starters and Kentucky's all-white team. Although the game is considered a milestone in racial integration, most of the players were only focused on winning the championship.

North Carolina State coach Jim Valvano rejoices after his Wolfpack pulled off one of the title game's biggest surprises, shooting down the top-ranked, high-flying, rim-rattling dunkers from Houston, 54–52, in 1983.

Georgetown's Patrick Ewing (33) snares a rebound in front of Villanova's Ed Pinckney in the 1985 title game. Despite being seeded 8th, Villanova upset top-ranked Georgetown by making 22 of 28 shots in a 66–64 stunner.

UCLA's Lew Alcindor grabs a rebound from Houston's Elvin Hayes in the Astrodome in a regular season game in front of a record 52,693 fans in 1968. Houston won, 71–69, but UCLA got its revenge later in the NCAA semi-finals, crushing the Cougars, 101–69.

For the 2006 tournament, the Boston College Eagles show off their Mr. Clean look. All but one player shaved their heads before their opener for good luck. It worked, because they came from behind to whip Pacific, 88–76.

The George Mason Patriots celebrate their 86–84 upset over the favored Connecticut Huskies in a 2006 regional final. As the No. 11 seed, George Mason became the lowest seeded team to reach the Final Four, matching LSU's improbable run of 1986.

Bisons senior guard Kevin Bettencourt.

A Dream Come True

While they were growing up in Gastonia, North Carolina, James Worthy and Eric "Sleepy" Floyd played basketball together. They dreamed of one day playing for the NCAA national championship.

They had no idea that their dream would actually come true—but with a twist.

As teenagers they played basketball for different high schools. Worthy attended Ashbrook High in Gastonia while Floyd went to Hunter Huss High. When Worthy was a sophomore and Floyd a junior, they played on their respective schools' teams for the state championship, which Hunter Huss won, 60–59.

After high school, they both went to college—Worthy to North Carolina and Floyd to Georgetown—on basketball scholarships and became All-Americans.

In 1982, the Gastonia-bred friends realized their dream when Georgetown met North Carolina for the national championship. This time Worthy got even for that one-point loss in the high school title game with a one-point win for the NCAA crown. Scoring a game-high 28 points, he led the Tar Heels to a 63–62 victory over Georgetown and his buddy Floyd, who scored 18 points.

BIRD MAN

*For the 1979 classic championship clash between Magic
Johnson's Michigan State Spartans and Larry Bird's
Indiana State Sycamores, ISU fans wore buttons pro-
claiming, "The state Bird of Indiana is Larry."*

*Maybe so, but the state hero of Michigan was
Johnson, who outscored Bird, 24–19, while leading the
Spartans to a 75–64 championship victory in what is still
the NCAA's highest-rated title game ever (24.1 television
rating; 38 share).*

Going Hog Wild

Bill Clinton was the first sitting president to attend Final
Four games as he cheered on his beloved Arkansas
Razorbacks when they won the 1994 championship.

In between affairs of state, the former Arkansas governor followed the team's run for the title on television. He
was so engrossed in the Razorbacks that he landed on the
cover of *Sports Illustrated* headlined "Whoooo, Pig,
Sooey!"

When the Razorbacks made it to the Elite Eight,
Clinton flew to Dallas, where he watched them defeat
Michigan, 76–68, in the Midwest Regional final. On the
floor afterwards, the president exchanged high-fives with
the players.

The following week, he took Air Force One to Charlotte for the Final Four games.

Arkansas, relying on its "40 minutes of hell" full-court press, wore down Arizona, 91–82, to set up the title match with Duke, which was gunning for its third title in four years.

From the skybox, Clinton whooped and hollered as Scotty Thurman's three-pointer with 50 seconds left broke a 70–70 tie and propelled the Razorbacks to a 76–72 triumph for the championship.

"I kept screaming to get the ball to Thurman," said Clinton. After the game, he exchanged hugs with Arkansas coach Nolan Richardson.

A few months later, the President honored the team at a Rose Garden ceremony. He told them, "I never did anything quite so crazy as to risk the 51 electoral votes of Michigan, Arizona, and North Carolina all in a row by going to those games. And when one of the reporters asked me about it when I got back, I said, 'If you'd been waiting for this as long as we have, it would be worth it all, including that.'"

A CHEER FOR THE CHEERLEADERS

For most of its 1964 national semifinal game, the UCLA Bruins were without their cheerleaders, who had been delayed by bad weather from getting to Kansas City's Municipal Auditorium. The Bruins trailed the Kansas State Wildcats, 75–70, with 7:28 remaining when the pumped-up UCLA cheerleaders, clad in their revealing (for that time) miniskirts, stormed into the arena.

Suddenly, UCLA caught fire and ripped off 11 straight points in less than three minutes and won, 90–84. The local newspapers quoted some of the players as saying the arrival of the cheerleaders was the spark that ignited their winning spurt. The next night, the Bruins blasted Duke, 98–83, for the title.

Let's Hear It for the Band

When the University of California Bears won the 1959 national championship, Coach Pete Newell was the first to claim the school's band deserved some of the credit.

The free-spirited Straw Hat Band did more than just play music. Its members stood in the student rooting section, filling Harmon Gym with goofy cheers and razor-sharp catcalls that often flustered opposing teams. During half times at basketball games, the Straw Hat Band entertained the fans by performing skits, gags, and Spike

Jones–style parodies.

The band sometimes went to away games to support the team. But its most famous contribution was helping the Bears in the 1959 Final Four. Thirty Straw Hatters flew to Louisville to support California in its semifinal contest against the favored Cincinnati Bearcats. Freedom Hall was packed with fans from nearby Cincinnati who tried to drown out the small band. But when Cal beat the Bearcats, 64–58, the Straw Hat Band's gleeful playing of its school's fight song was clearly heard by the glum Cincinnati fans as they filed silently out of the arena.

The next day, Coach Newell invited the Straw Hatters to eat with the team. He recalled, "Not only did I appreciate their effort, I felt our team needed to relax. This was no time for a quiet meal."

In the other semifinal the night before, the hometown favorite Louisville Cardinals had been shot down, 94–79, by the Jerry West–led West Virginia Mountaineers. As a result, the championship game between Cal and West Virginia wasn't expected to draw as many rabid fans. Relatively few from California had the time or money to make it to Louisville.

So the Straw Hat Band had an ingenious plan to sway the mostly neutral crowd to root for the Bears. Hours before the big game, the band played at several venues throughout Louisville and primed the locals to support Cal. The big push to woo the fans came during the pre-game festivities. Band member Elton Butler went on the public address system and expressed the Straw Hatters's thanks for Louisville's hospitality. The band then pranced into the arena playing an upbeat "My Old Kentucky Home." The crowd went wild. "That entrance was worth inspirational points," Newell said later. "We felt we had inherited the home court advantage."

Now that the band had won over most of the fans to the Cal side, the crowd cheered the Bears to the national championship, 71–70.

When reporters asked Coach Newell the secret to his team's success, he replied, "The Straw Hat Band. They say home court advantage is worth 10 points to a basketball team. If so, the Hatters have been worth 11 points to us on the road."

"After we bring in the tanks and armor?"
—Fairleigh Davidson coach Tom Green, when asked what his 16th-seeded team's strategy was before it lost to top-seeded Illinois, 67–55, in 2005

UNDERDOGS
AND UPSETS

Spider Bites

The Richmond Spiders have a bite that has made them
giant killers in the NCAA Tournament. They are the only
team to have won opening round games while seeded
15th, 14th, 13th, and 12th.

The Spiders pulled off their most shocking upset at
College Park, Maryland, when they stunned hoops powerhouse Syracuse, 73–69, in 1991. It was the first time in
tournament history that a No. 15 seed had beaten a No. 2
seed. (As of 2006, a No. 16 seed had yet to win a game.)

The Spiders jumped to an early lead over the seventh-
ranked Orangemen and never trailed in the contest. Curtis

Blair led a balanced Richmond attack with 18 points and six assists, while Terry "Super Sub" Connolly tallied 14 points, seven boards and five assists.

Syracuse's Billy Owens, who scored 22 points, hit a basket with 32 seconds left to pull the Orangemen to within one. But Richmond made three free throws in the final seconds—two by freshman Eugene Burroughs—to clinch the upset. Unfortunately, the Spiders fell to No. 10 seed Temple, 77–64, in the second round.

Richmond began building its reputation as a bookie-busting team in 1984 when, as a No. 12 seed, it nipped the fifth-seeded Auburn Tigers, 71–70. Back then, the NCAA had play-in games for the tag-along teams. The Spiders had to play in one of those contests—an 89–65 victory over Rider—just to get the chance to face Auburn.

Although the Tigers featured future NBA stars Charles Barkley and Chuck Person, the Spiders had Johnny Newman, a future professional as well, and he helped boost his team to a 17-point halftime lead. Auburn mounted a furious comeback but Richmond, behind Newman's 26 points, didn't cave. Alas, Indiana beat the Spiders in the next round, 75–67.

Four years later, the Spiders faced the Hoosiers in a 13th-seed vs. 4th-seed matchup. Never mind that Indiana had won the national title the previous year; it was payback time for Richmond.

Against the Hoosiers, Richmond's Rodney Rice scored 21 points, including a jumper with less than a minute to play, which gave the Spiders the lead for good, 70–69. Indiana's Keith Smart, who hit a last-second jumper for the national title the previous year, tried to be the hero again. But his shot with 20 seconds left was off the mark. Rice's rebound fed a fast break bucket by Ken Atkinson to close out a 72–69 history-making win.

It was only the second time ever that a defending national champion had been ousted in its tourney opener. (The first was defending titlist Louisville which, in 1981, lost to Arkansas, 74–73, when U.S. Reid heaved in a half-court shot at the buzzer.) The Spiders's victory avenged two previous postseason losses to Indiana.

Then the underdogs, paced by Peter Woolfolks's 27 points, surprised No. 5 seed Georgia Tech, 59–55, in the second round to advance to their first ever NCAA Sweet Sixteen. The Spiders's tourney dreams ended when they fell to the nation's top-ranked team, Temple, 69–47.

In 1998, Richmond engineered another upset special in the opening round when, as a No. 14 seed, it edged the third-seeded South Carolina Gamecocks, 62–61. The Spiders overcame a 37 percent shooting performance by relying on Marseilles Brown's five three-pointers in the first half, Jarod Stevenson's 24 points, and clutch six-for-six free-throw shooting down the stretch. Richmond then lost, 81–66, to Washington in the next round.

So why were the Spiders so dangerous in the opening round? One reason might have been their coach, Dick Tarrant, who was a master at getting the most out of his players against overwhelming odds. He learned a thing or two about motivation from the coach of the freshman basketball team that he was on when he attended Fordham— some guy named Vince Lombardi.

"It's very psychological. In a forty-minute game, anybody can beat anybody."
—Arizona assistant coach and former Wildcat player Josh Pastner

Bucking the Odds

The odds that the Santa Clara University Broncos could take out the Arizona Wildcats in the opening round of the 1993 tournament were stacked higher than a Big Sur cliff. Las Vegas had the small California Jesuit school a 20-point underdog. Tournament officials had seeded them 15th and the Wildcats second. Oddsmakers had listed Santa Clara an 8-million-to-1 long shot to win the title and Arizona's chances at 7-to-1.

The Broncos got no respect, at least not from the *St.*

Louis Post Dispatch, which described them as "a motley jumble of eggheads, surfers, and imports."

Somehow, some way, the Broncos reared up and stomped the fifth-ranked team in the nation in a colossal shocker, 64–61. In terms of a point spread, it's the biggest upset in NCAA playoff history and the second of only four times that a No. 15 seed beat a No. 2 seed.

"Well, it didn't hurt to get a little lucky," recalled Dick Davey, who was in his first year as head coach of Santa Clara. "I mean, we went about forty minutes without scoring." He wasn't talking about the game clock, but rather the actual time, although he exaggerated a bit.

The Broncos had astonished everyone by galloping out to a 14-point lead with about five minutes remaining in the first half. The next time they scored, however, they were down by 11 points in the second half. Arizona, fueled by future NBA stars Chris Mills, Damon Stoudamire and Khalid Reeves, had gone on a 25–0 rampage.

In an interview with John Blanchette of the *Spokane* (Washington) *Spokesman Review,* Davey said that during the run, "I took a time-out, because as a coach you're supposed to do that in that situation. And we sat there for two minutes and nobody said a word. I couldn't think of anything to say to them. Finally, I said, 'Gentlemen, we have to score.' Which just goes to show you how valuable good coaching is."

The Broncos slipped to 13 points behind before they mounted their comeback, which got a lift when the Vanderbilt band, whose team would be playing next in the Salt Lake City arena, adopted them and helped get the crowd behind them. Santa Clara finally took the lead late in the game and held on as Stoudamire's desperate last-second three-pointer to tie the game clanked off the rim.

"The difference? We had Steve Nash," Davey said. Nash, who would become an NBA MVP, was a 6-foot-5 freshman who showed remarkable poise by making six straight free throws down the stretch.

"You know, occasionally you get lucky," Davey conceded. "We had good leadership from our point guard, John Woolery, a fellow who could handle the pressure.

"But really, for a fifteen to beat a two, you've got to be a little lucky, make some shots—and believe in yourself."

Davey said that as he was walking off the court after the game, Woolery was talking to a dejected Chris Mills. "Mills had his head down," Davey recalled, "and John slapped him on the back and said, 'Don't get too down. Next year, you'll be playing for a lot of money [in the NBA] and I'll be working at some job.'"

Ya Gotta Believe

In the opening round of the 1997 East Regional, the No. 15 seed Coppin State Eagles were 20-point underdogs to the No. 2 seed South Carolina Gamecocks.

That didn't seem to matter to the players from the small Baltimore school. They believed in themselves when no one else did. But who could blame the naysayers. Coppin State had never won a game in an NCAA Tournament. Only twice before, since the tourney was seeded in 1979, had a No. 15 seed beaten a No. 2 seed. The Eagles weren't ranked and came from the Mid-Eastern Athletic Conference, which was 0–15 in tournament history.

The Gamecocks were ranked sixth in the nation and belonged to the prestigious Southeastern Conference. On the eve of the game, ESPN analyst Dale Brown said Coppin State's guards lacked the talent and toughness to keep pace with South Carolina's great backcourt trio of Larry Davis, B.J. McKie, and Melvin Watson.

Making things even grimmer, the Eagles' best player, Terquin Mott, sprained his ankle the day before the game. As if that weren't enough, when Coppin State's team and entourage left their hotel for the Pittsburgh Civic Center, the hotel staff started turning over many of their rooms to other guests, anticipating a romp for South Carolina.

And yet the Eagles believed.

"We approached the game as it being winnable," said Coach Ron "Fang" Mitchell. "I think the difference for us was we weren't just happy to be there. For a lot of the lower seeds, just making the tournament seems to complete their goal. Not us. We wanted to win."

Right before the tip-off, Mitchell said, he looked into his players' eyes, and he liked what he saw. They were the looks of winners.

Even when the Eagles fell behind by seven points in the second half, they believed in themselves. They stormed back and, with Danny Singletary's 22 points leading the way, they walloped South Carolina, 78–65. It was the largest margin of victory ever for a No. 15 seed.

Afterwards, Gamecocks coach Eddie Fogler was gracious in defeat. "Congratulations to Coppin State," he said. "Without a doubt, they were easily the better team today."

Coppin State almost pulled off another huge upset two days later, but lost to Texas, 82–81.

According to Clay Latimer of the *Rocky Mountain* (Colorado) *News*, after the South Carolina game, Eagles center Terquin Mott stood outside the team's giddy locker room, trying to put this sweet victory into some sort of perspective. At that moment, Coach Mitchell's wife,

Yvonne, handed Mott a Bible. She told him to turn to Chapter 17 of the First Book of Samuel, verses 20 through 54. It was the story of David and Goliath.

Hampton's Impressive Debut

In its first NCAA Tournament ever, No. 15 seed Hampton—a small Virginia school—shocked the No. 2 seed, nationally-ranked Iowa State Cyclones, 58–57, in the opening round of the 2001 playoffs in Boise, Idaho.

"I don't know if magic was in the air; our kids just believed," Hampton coach Steve Merfeld said. "But when it actually happened, for me it was like an out-of-body experience."

When the upstart Pirates made their move from an 11-point second-half deficit, the once-neutral crowd took a liking to Hampton, its cheerleaders, and its band until the Boise arena seemed like the underdogs' home court.

The Pirates rallied while holding the Cyclones scoreless for the final seven minutes. Hampton's Tarvis Williams flipped in a four-footer in the lane with 6.9 seconds remaining for the winning points. Iowa State's Jamaal Tinsley took the ball down court but missed a layup with 1.2 seconds to go, setting off a mid-court frenzy as the Pirates and their fans swarmed the floor.

Hampton player David Johnson picked up Merfeld

and carried him around the court as the coach happily pumped his fists and kicked his legs.

"I don't remember anything about my initial reactions," Merfeld told Tim May of the *Columbus* (Ohio) *Dispatch*. "My memory picks up when David Johnson was holding me and saying, 'I've gotcha, Coach. I've gotcha.'"

DID YOU KNOW . . .

- Marseilles Brown, the 5-foot-6 point guard who fed Williams for his game-winning basket, was involved in an earlier classic postseason upset. He also played for Richmond when the No. 14 seed Spiders upset No. 3 seed South Carolina in the first round of the 1998 tourney.
- Hampton's band and cheerleaders made such an impression on the Boise crowd that they were asked to perform between periods at a minor-league hockey game the following night. The band wowed the spectators, who booed when the hockey game resumed because they wanted to see more of Hampton's music makers.

A Most Upsetting Day

March 14, 1986, was one of the most upsetting days in NCAA Tournament history. That's the date two No. 14 seeds each beat a No. 3 in the opening round. Even more astonishing, the wins by the virtually unknown teams came at the expense of two storied athletic programs—Indiana and Notre Dame.

The mighty Hoosiers, whose year was being chronicled by sportswriter John Feinstein for his book, *Season on the Brink,* saw their season end prematurely and ingloriously in Syracuse when the Cleveland State Vikings sacked them, 83–79.

Playing a fast-paced, pressing brand of basketball known as the run-and-stun, the starless Vikings became an instant hit with hoops fans outside the Hoosier state. Among their starters were freshman guard Ken "Mouse" McFadden—a native of Queens, N.Y., who never played high school basketball—and Eric Mudd, a senior center who joined the team only after his aunt talked Coach Kevin Mackey into giving him a chance to play.

From the opening tip-off, Cleveland State grabbed an early lead that it never relinquished and ran Indiana ragged. Coach Bobby Knight and his star, Steve Alford, had no answer for the Vikings and high scorer Clinton Ransey (27 points).

Interestingly, Coach Knight knew two days before that his team was ripe for an upset. After watching Cleveland State game film, he turned to his assistants and said, "We've got a real problem. This team we're watching here can beat us. Their press will give us trouble. But there's absolutely no way we're going to convince the players of that until we're about ten points down."

Cleveland State was no fluke. It beat No. 6 seed St. Joseph's in the next round, 75–69. But then the Cinderella team lost a Sweet Sixteen heartbreaker to Navy, 71–70, on David Robinson's winning shot with five seconds left. Cleveland State is the only school seeded in the bottom quarter of a bracket (13 through 16) to reach the Sweet Sixteen.

***

The same day as the Vikings' surprise victory over Indiana, the University of Arkansas–Little Rock Trojans pulled off an identical upset, a 90–83 stunner over Notre Dame, which was ranked tenth in the nation.

The 22-11 Trojans, 17-point underdogs who had never been to the Big Dance before, were such unknowns that they hadn't even been seen on statewide television until their last regular season game. But they made a name for themselves by knocking off Digger Phelps's Fighting Irish while the Metrodome crowd in Minneapolis howled with glee.

Shooting at better than 60 percent for the entire game,

the Trojans didn't fold during crunch time, making nine of 11 foul shots while forcing Notre Dame into several crucial turnovers. The Trojans's Pete Myers and Michael Clarke led the way with 29 and 27 points, respectively.

After dispatching Notre Dame, the Trojans put up a fierce fight against North Carolina State before succumbing in double overtime, 80–66.

Heady Rush to Judgment

ESPN analyst and motormouth Dick Vitale has never been afraid to say what's on his mind. He'll stand by his words—even when it means he must eat crow.

In 1987, when No. 14 seed Austin Peay faced No. 3 seed Illinois in the opening round of the 1987 tournament, Vitale predicted that the high-flying Illini—led by Kendall Gill, Nick Anderson, and Ken Norman—would crush the Governors and ultimately reach the Final Four.

But Austin Peay could care less what Vitale thought. The team employed what its coach, Lake Kelly, called the "Sic 'em" offense: "I just throw the ball out and say 'Sic 'em.'"

To most everyone's surprise, especially the Illini, the unheralded Governors were holding their own in the game, which was televised by ESPN. In the second half, Austin Peay trailed Illinois by only three points, when

Vitale appeared in ESPN's studio and bellowed to the television audience, "There's no way Illinois loses this game! If Illinois loses, I'll stand on my head!"

It was a declaration he shouldn't have made, because Austin Peay edged Illinois, 68–67, in one of the top upsets in playoff history. (The Governors then lost to eventual Final Four participant Providence in overtime, 90–87.)

Being a man of his word, Vitale traveled to Austin Peay's campus in Clarksville, Tennessee, and successfully stood on his head for ten seconds.

DEFLATING BIG O'S EGO

As the California Bears lined up against the favored Cincinnati Bearcats for the national semifinal tip-off of the 1959 tournament, Cal forward Bob Dalton faced Oscar Robertson, who had been named College Player of the Year for the second season in a row. The future Hall of Famer also was among the nation's top scorers, averaging 32.6 points per game for the 26-4 Bearcats.

Dalton extended his hand to Robertson and said with a straight face, "My name's Dalton. What's yours?" Big O seemed taken aback as he blankly shook his opponent's hand. Whether or not that bit of gamesmanship worked, Robertson had an off day as Dalton held him to 19 points on just five field goals in Cal's unexpected 64–58 victory. The next day, the Bears edged West Virginia, 71–70, to claim the national championship.

Cutting It Close

It seemed obvious who would win when Big Ten tournament champ Iowa, a No. 3 seed, jumped out to a 17-point cushion over No. 14 seed Northwestern State with less than nine minutes left in a 2006 opening round game at Auburn Hills, Michigan. Besides, the out-of-the-way school from Natchitoches, Louisiana, had never beaten a team like the 15th-ranked Hawkeyes in its history.

Funny how things work out.

The Demons weren't fazed when they were down 54–37 with 8:30 remaining. Six times during the regular season they had rallied to win after falling behind by double digits, so they figured they could do it again. And they did, but they sure cut it close, winning an amazing 64–63 upset on a three-pointer with just a half second left.

"We didn't panic," forward Jermaine Spencer said after the game. "We have seven seniors. We had been in that situation before. We had to calm down and be patient. We played twelve people and you could see them [the Hawkeyes] getting tired. We just wore them down."

"We never thought we weren't going to win," added Demons guard Clifton Lee, who scored 18 points, including four second-half three-pointers. "We've come back before in big games, but I guess this was the biggest one so far."

After Northwestern State outscored the Hawkeyes, 24–9, in the closing minutes, the Demons were still down, 63–61. It looked like they had run out of time after Kerwin Forges's attempt at a game-winner from beyond the arc banged off the hoop with four seconds left. However, teammate Jermaine Wallace chased down the rebound and dribbled to the left corner. As the Iowa defenders scrambled toward him, he launched a fade-away jumper a fraction of a second before the buzzer and watched it rattle through the hoop.

"When I saw the ball leave his hand, I stared it down," teammate Colby Bargeman told reporters. "I just knew it was going to go in. I just started jumping up and down and just screaming and hollering. It was unbelievable."

When he returned to his hotel room, Bargeman was still too pumped up to sleep. "I kept watching the replay over and over on TV," he said. "This was one of the greatest games in NCAA Tournament history. It's great to be a part of it."

The victory validated Coach Mike McConathy's decision to load Northwestern State's non-conference schedule with teams from major conferences to prepare his squad for the tourney.

The Demons were the first Southland Conference team to advance since Karl Malone and Louisiana Tech reached the Sweet Sixteen in 1985. During practice the day before the Iowa game, Detroit Pistons executive Joe Dumars, who graduated from Southland's McNeese State in 1985, gave the Demons an inspirational message. "He said the name on the jerseys doesn't matter," recalled Lee. "He said small-town kids can make it big."

Added teammate Tyronn Mitchell, who helped a defensive effort that forced 15 turnovers, "We've been playing from behind all year long. When we lead at the half, it seems like we tend to lose the game. So, when we were down four at the half, I felt good about our chances."

They didn't feel too good in the second round when Northwestern State trailed No. 6 seed West Virginia, 41–19, at the half. Still, the Demons scrambled back to within eight before stalling out and falling to the Mountaineers, 67–54.

"You go from the top of the world to the bottom of the trash barrel, but that's okay," said McConathy. "I'm proud of these guys."

DID YOU KNOW . . .
- Iowa coach Steve Alford was painfully aware of how a No. 14 seed can beat a No. 3 seed. It happened to him in 1986 as a player for Indiana when it was upset by Cleveland State, 83–79.

Experience Doesn't Always Count

The No. 14 seed Bucknell Bison trampled the No. 3 seed Kansas Jayhawks, 64–63, in the first round of the 2005 playoffs.

What was so extraordinary about the upset was that Kansas—one of basketball's premier programs—featured a senior class that had been to two Final Fours and an Elite Eight and was led by a first-team All-American, Wayne Simien. And the Jayhawks were ranked tenth in the nation. Unranked Bucknell, which had only one senior, competed in the the Patriot League, whose teams had never won a tournament game. Academics were such a top priority at the Lewisburg, Pennsylvania, school that its best player, Chris McNaughton, missed the start of practice for the Kansas game because he was busy in an electrical engineering laboratory.

Bucknell's victory was its first in NCAA Tournament play and its biggest triumph ever in the 110-year history of the school. The Bison (23-9) snapped a streak of 21 consecutive first-round victories for Kansas, which was playing in its 107th tournament game—fourth most in NCAA history.

Bucknell grounded the Jayhawks, despite making only 40 percent of its shots. But the Bison had only nine turnovers, and they played defense well enough to force

Kansas into missing its last 10 shots. All 14 of the Jayhawks's points in the final eight minutes came from the free-throw line.

McNaughton, a 6-foot-11 sophomore center from Germany, banked in the winning basket with a little jump hook in the lane with 10.5 seconds remaining. A last-ditch Kansas shot clanged off the rim, triggering joyous pandemonium on the court for the Bison and their fans at the Ford Center in Oklahoma City.

"It was just so exciting," guard Kevin Bettencourt said. "To see how hard we had to work to get to this point. We would not have been satisfied just to be here. We wanted to win. It was unbelievable."

Said Bucknell coach Pat Flannery, "You look at Kansas, and it [the upset] is almost surreal. Certainly, this is the biggest win we've ever had, and I'm happy for the Patriot League.

"This was a great college game, and to coach in it was an honor. I'm so proud of these kids. We battled all night and made Kansas work for everything they got. We really competed. Every time it looked like they were going to stretch their lead, we responded."

Unfortunately, Bucknell lost in the next round to Wisconsin, 71–62.

DID YOU KNOW . . .

- According to federal filings, Bucknell spent $900,000 on its basketball program in the 2005-06 season. Kansas spent $3.9 million.
- For beating Kansas, Bucknell was named the recipient of ESPN'S 2005 ESPY Award in the "Best Upset" category.

For Pete's Sake

If ever there was a tournament game that the Princeton Tigers wanted to win, it was the 1996 opening round clash with defending national champion UCLA.

They wanted to win for their long-time coach Pete Carril, who had announced he was retiring after 29 years at the Ivy League school.

But a victory over the Bruins was a tall order for a team that had a reputation for coming up short in close games, having lost its previous four NCAA Tournament games by a combined 15 points. UCLA was seeded fourth; Princeton a lowly 13th when they met at the RCA Dome in Indianapolis.

"Our team had never beaten anyone of that stature," player Sydney Johnson told Princeton sportswriter Jerry Price years later. "Back then, Princeton was known for coming close. Although we didn't think we were going to win, we knew we had a chance with the game plan that was put together and the fact that we had nothing to lose."

The Tigers quickly fell behind 7–0 before the first TV time-out. But they didn't panic. With a patient, deliberate offense and a tenacious defense, Princeton trailed by only one, 19–18, at the half. The Bruins were so troubled by the score that they stayed in the locker room until the last possible moment, trying to figure out how to solve the Tigers's defense.

Although there were few fans from Princeton, the crowd—mostly backers from other teams that had played earlier in the day—jumped to the Tigers's side. "As we made a game of it, they started to realize just how big an upset they might be watching," Johnson recalled. "The place was so loud, and I think the noise started to take some of the spirit out of UCLA."

Neither team led by more than three points until the Bruins pulled away to a 41–34 advantage with less than seven minutes remaining. Then came the turning point. After a Princeton turnover, UCLA's Toby Bailey threw a three-quarter-length pass to Ed O'Bannon for what should have been a cinch layup that would have demoralized the Tigers. But he blew the easy bucket, giving Princeton new life.

Johnson then nailed a three-pointer, Steve Goodrich

made a reverse layup, and, following a steal, Johnson scored on another layup that tied the game, 41–41, with 2:58 to go as the Dome crowd roared its approval. After both teams failed to score on their next two possessions, Princeton had the ball and called a time-out with 21 seconds left.

When play resumed, Johnson got the ball to Goodrich in the high post with 10 seconds left. Meanwhile, freshman Gabe Lewullis cut from the wing to the basket, ran back to the wing, and then doubled back to take a perfect feed from Goodrich. Lewullis made the layup with 3.9 seconds left. It was the classic back-door play. The Bruins in-bounded the ball and called time-out with 1.7 seconds showing on the clock.

Wrote Price, "The game was then delayed for more than seven minutes while the officials decided to put 2.2 seconds on the clock and award UCLA the ball in the front court. UCLA and Princeton then called separate time-outs, increasing the tension and leaving the crowd to wonder if this might not end up as the cruelest night of them all for Princeton." After all, Princeton was the team that seemed to always lose the close games.

But not this time. The celebration began after UCLA's Toby Bailey took the inbounds pass and, with Johnson guarding him, put up an air ball as the horn sounded.

Incredibly, Princeton had shut out UCLA over the final 6:30 in another remarkable NCAA Tournament upset.

"I worked at CBS for a long time, covered hundreds and hundreds of events," said Andrea Joyce, who was the sideline reporter for the network in the Dome that night. "The Princeton-UCLA game was without a doubt the highlight."

"A lot of times in this day and age, athletes, particularly young athletes, are afraid to show emotion," Joyce told Price. "I was so struck by this group of guys who were so genuinely excited by what they had done and weren't afraid to show it. They were just so thrilled by the moment."

The euphoria ended two days later when Mississippi State shot down the Tigers, 63–41. But Princeton will always savor the UCLA upset—especially because it was the crowning achievement of a Hall of Fame career for Carril.

"I guess," Carril told Joyce on the court, moments after the game, "that I won't have to be known as the guy who lost every close one."

"To me, this is the greatest venue for sports fans. You've got new faces every year. Who's going to be the next Cinderella?"
—Valparaiso coach Homer Drew, talking about March Madness

THE GOOD, THE
BAD, AND THE UGLY

Breaking the Gentlemen's Agreement

During the 1950s and early 1960s, there had been a gentlemen's agreement among white coaches of racially integrated Division I teams that they would start no more than two blacks at home and, if necessary, three on the road. In 1954, University of San Francisco coach Phil Woolpert was one of the first to ignore that unwritten pact.

Although some colleges had integrated basketball teams in the 1940s, others, especially in the south, didn't put a black in their lineup until as late as the 1970s. As a result, integrated teams—even champions—were often wounded by the slings and arrows of racial prejudice.

USF, a small Jesuit school of 3,000 students that didn't even have a campus gym, was a powerhouse in basketball. Thanks to a then-record 60-game winning streak, the Dons won back-to-back national championships in 1955 and 1956. They were the kings of the court because their regular-season starting lineup included three incredibly talented blacks—Hal Perry and future NBA greats Bill Russell and K.C. Jones. "It was never said, but you knew as a coach that you had to be aware of the quota thing," said Woolpert.

Significantly, the coach started three blacks in 1954, the same year that the U.S. Supreme Court handed down its history-making Brown vs. Board of Education decision banning segregation in public schools. Bigots weren't happy with the Dons. One sportswriter referred to the team as "the Junior Globetrotters."

The Dons ran into racial problems at the then-prestigious All-College Invitational Tournament in Oklahoma City over the Christmas holiday during the 1954–55 season. When USF arrived at the tournament site, officials there said that black players weren't allowed in any of the downtown hotels that had booked the teams. The black players were supposed to stay in the empty dormitories on the local campus.

Hal Perry called a players-only meeting to discuss the situation and they emerged from their confab in unity. All the USF players, white and black alike, agreed to stay together as a team and bunk in the dorms that had been vacated by students for the holidays. Then the team went out and won the tourney, cracking the top 20 rankings for the first time that year.

They never lost again that season—and capped it off with a 77–63 triumph over La Salle to earn the 1955 national title. For the first time ever, three of the five starters on a major college championship team were African-American. The trio combined to score 51 points in the title game. The following year, when the Dons repeated as champs by downing Iowa, 83–71, four USF blacks played in the title game—Russell, Perry, Gene Brown and Warren Baxter, who combined to score 60 points.

DID YOU KNOW . . .
- City College of New York played three black players on its 1950 title-winning team, but only two were in the starting lineup.

Team Unity

The Kansas Jayhawks had a vile racial experience in the 1957 NCAA Midwest Regional in Dallas, which was the farthest south the players had been.

That season, Kansas featured two blacks—Wilt Chamberlain, the nation's most intimidating sophomore, and senior Maurice King. When the Jayhawks arrived in Dallas for the tourney, they learned that their hotel refused to check in any black guests.

Coach Dick Harp announced, "If we can't all stay together, none of us will be staying here. We're not going to put Maurice and Wilt in private homes." So he moved the entire team to a hotel in the suburb of Grand Prairie.

The hate-mongers were out in force, unleashing torrents of racial epithets at the two African-American players and at the other Jayhawks for being on a team with blacks. It turned so ugly that police were needed to escort the team on and off the basketball court and back to the airport.

But Kansas got even. The Jayhawks whipped Southern Methodist, 73–65, and then vanquished Oklahoma City, 81–61, and San Francisco, 80–56, to reach the championship game. Unfortunately, the Jayhawks lost to North Carolina, 54–53 in triple overtime.

DID YOU KNOW . . .

- The University of California was the last all-white team to win the NCAA championship. Without any blacks on its roster, the Bears eked past West Virginia, 71–70, for the 1959 title.
- In 1950, when all-white Kentucky lost to City College of New York's integrated team, Kentucky's legislature considered flying the state flag at the state capitol at half-staff.

Victory for Equality

The Loyola Ramblers and the Mississippi State Bulldogs struck a historic blow for social justice in a 1963 tournament game at a time when the civil rights movement was gaining momentum.

During the 1962–63 season, Loyola coach George Ireland disregarded the unwritten rule among white coaches to start no more than three blacks. He inserted four blacks in his starting lineup because, he said, they were his best players. The Ramblers made history that season in a game against Wyoming when they became the first Division I team ever to start five black players in a game—Vic Rouse, Les Hunter, Ron Miller, Jerry Harkness, and Rich Rochelle.

Racists spewed their hatred when the team from Chicago ventured below the Mason-Dixon Line. After a tough game against Marshall in Huntington, West Virginia, the Ramblers had to sneak out of their locker room through a back door to avoid an angry mob. In Houston, the team was spit on and targeted by penny-throwing spectators, and the black players were denied service in restaurants. In New Orleans, the black players were forced to bunk with black families while the white teammates stayed at a hotel. John Egan, the team's point guard and lone white starter, was frequently called an "albino" and "traitor" by bigoted fans, some waving Confederate flags.

"It was taxing on our minds to go into a place like Houston and have them throwing stuff at you and cursing and spitting," Hunter recalled to Paul Kuharsky of Nashville's *The Tennessean*. "That kind of fueled the black guys. I know it fueled me to play a little bit harder when we came up against an all-white team. I think Ireland used that to his advantage, too: 'Let's show these guys down here.' He was talking as if he was a black guy, also."

Led by 6-foot-2 star Jerry Harkness, the Ramblers lost only two games that season. For the Mideast Regional semifinals at East Lansing, Michigan, the Ramblers were scheduled to play Southeastern Conference champion

Mississippi State.

Even though the Bulldogs had won the SEC title in three of the previous four years and received automatic bids to the tourney, they were barred from going by an unwritten Mississippi policy that forbid state schools from competing against integrated teams. As a result, SEC runner-up Kentucky had represented the conference.

This prejudiced principle had never been tested until MSU's coach Babe McCarthy and school president Dr. D.W. Colvard—the first non-Mississippian president in the university's 82-year history—courageously took a stand. They chose to defy intolerant legislators and compete against racially mixed Loyola in East Lansing and face the consequences later in the powder keg of Starkville.

The Bulldogs definitely wanted to play Loyola. "I don't see anything morally wrong with playing against Negroes, Indians, Russians, or any other race or nationality," said forward Leland Mitchell.

Mississippi Governor Ross R. Barnett, a segregationist who actively opposed the integration of the University of Mississippi by James Meredith in 1962, forbade the Bulldogs from traveling to the tournament. Adding muscle to the ban, two segregationist state legislators drew up injunction papers seeking to prohibit the team from leaving Mississippi and using state funds to travel. Billy Mitts, one of the "Jim Crow" state senators, was a former Mississippi State student body president.

Dr. Colvard was swamped with hate mail. Typical was a letter from a woman from Ashland, Mississippi, who wrote, "For a coach to insult those white boys by asking them to play against negros [sic] is most disgusting."

An editor of the *Jackson* (Mississippi) *Daily News* wrote that "a crack at a mythical national championship isn't worth subjecting young Mississippians to the switch-blade knife society that integration inevitably spawns."

McCarthy and Dr. Colvard concocted a plan to spirit the players out of town in the middle of the night. The clever scheme involved a series of strategic moves, including the deployment of a decoy team to trick state police.

In Roy Neel's *Dynamite! 75 Years of Vanderbilt Basketball*, Bo Carter, a one-time assistant sports information director at MSU, recalled, "Local sheriffs and state troopers were instructed to serve injunctions on McCarthy to prevent his departure for the tournament. Coach McCarthy sent all the players to private homes around Starkville to keep them under wraps until it was time to leave. Then, McCarthy and his assistant coach drove to Nashville and hid out in a hotel. At an appointed time, all the players met at the Columbus [Mississippi] airport."

Fortunately, a sheriff's deputy who was supposed to

make sure none of the players tried to leave town by plane was sympathetic to their cause. He conveniently left the airport minutes before the players arrived and avoided what could have been an ugly scene. They flew to Nashville to meet McCarthy, who then loaded everyone on a charter flight to East Lansing.

"The Bulldogs were the attraction of the tournament. Everyone congratulated them on their escape from Starkville," said Carter. "It was like a spy movie."

Upon Mississippi State's arrival at East Lansing, McCarthy told reporters, "I'm happy my boys could come just to see a team like Loyola play."

Of course, the Bulldogs didn't travel that distance and risk the wrath of racist politicians and back-home bigots just to watch the nation's highest-scoring team. MSU was out to beat the Ramblers . . . and make a social statement.

When Harkness, who was Loyola's captain, shook hands with Mississippi State captain Joe Dan Gold before the game, flashbulbs popped throughout the field house. "I couldn't imagine what was going on," Harkness recalled. To him and his teammates, it was just another game that the Ramblers needed to win to advance in the tournament.

Playing methodically, Mississippi State slowed down Loyola's well-oiled scoring machine, but still tumbled,

61–51. In truth, this was one contest in which the outcome seemed secondary to the fact the game was played at all.

Loyola went on to win the 1963 NCAA title by upsetting the two-time defending champion Cincinnati Bearcats, 60–58, in overtime.

When the Bulldogs's plane returned to Starkville, 700 people greeted the squad. "We saw the lines of cars backed up from the airport," player Doug Hutton recalled in a *Sports Illustrated* story years later. "Then someone said, 'Do you reckon they're here to welcome us back, or send us back?' But over all these years, I don't know that any of us have heard any negative comments."

According to a poll conducted by a Jackson, Mississippi, TV station, more than eight out of ten people were in favor of the team playing Loyola.

The game didn't change the hearts of racist students. They distributed a flyer around campus that said, "Niggers 61–Nigger lovers 51. MSU, being the first Mississippi school to be defeated by a bunch of niggers, has caused our forefathers to turn over in their graves."

However, Robert Taylor, MSU's student body president, wrote Ireland a letter of congratulations after Loyola won the championship. It said, in part, "All the students at Mississippi State were rooting for you in the NCAA tournament and were overjoyed when your team made the magnificent comeback to beat Cincinnati. We were honored to have played you and look forward to meeting you again."

Two years later, Richard Holmes, the foster son of a Starkville physician, integrated the Mississippi State campus without incident.

DID YOU KNOW . . .

- After 1963, Mississippi State didn't appear in the NCAA Tournament again until 1991, when the Bulldogs' 13-man roster had 10 blacks.
- Of all the starters in the 1963 championship contest, Loyola had four blacks and Cincinnati had three. It was the first time a majority of blacks started in a title game.

It's All Black and White

The 1966 title game between the Texas Western Miners's all-black starting lineup and the Kentucky Wildcats's all-white team proved a milestone in racial integration throughout college athletics.

But, at the time, most of the players didn't see it that way. They were out to win the championship.

Miners guard Willie Worsley said he never thought about the social magnitude of the game when he stepped onto the court in College Park, Maryland. All he felt was excitement over playing in a championship contest that was nationally televised so all his friends and relatives back in New York City could watch him.

Texas Western coach Don Haskins has said, "I really didn't think about starting five black guys. I just wanted to put my five best guys on the court."

His five best guys—Worsley, Harry Flournoy, David Lattin, Bobby Joe Hill, and Orsten Artis—were good enough to beat top-ranked, lily-white Kentucky, 72–65.

But whether or not the Miners considered the game groundbreaking, they certainly were aware of a racial divide in basketball at that time, especially in the South, where change came slow to college campuses.

So when 27-1 Texas Western—with seven blacks on the roster—took on 27-1 Kentucky, many people realized this would not be just another NCAA championship game. For some, it was a landmark for racial equality in college sports. For others, it was proof the country was going to hell in a basket. What happened that season for Texas Western (now known as the University of Texas-El Paso) was turned into the hit 2006 film, *Glory Road*.

The Miners played dogged defense and made 28 of 34

free throws. The turning point of the game came midway through the first half when Texas Western was leading, 10–9. Bobby Joe Hill stole the ball from Kentucky guard Tommy Kron, dribbled half the length of the court and made a layup. Seconds later, Hill did it again, this time to guard Louie Dampier, and went all the way for another uncontested layup. The Wildcats never recovered nor captured the lead.

For all the joy, pride, and satisfaction that Haskins felt over winning the title, there was a disturbing downside. Not until he returned to El Paso did the coach realize how outraged many people were over the triumph of his black starters.

"After a few days, the hate mail started coming and coming and coming," Haskins told Iliana Limon of the *Albuquerque* [New Mexico] *Tribune*. He estimated that about 40,000 pieces landed on his desk. Even more dismaying, he began receiving condemnations from African-American leaders, who accused the coach of exploiting black players to win a championship. Then there were the death threats—at least a dozen of them— from the lunatic fringe.

"I've never been more shocked in my life," Haskins recalled. "I said for a long time I was probably the least happy guy to ever win a national championship."

Haskins plays down his role in that championship season, but his players have said he protected them from almost all the angry letters, hurtful comments, and threats to gun down their coach.

"We were all in our own little niche," Worsley told Milan Simonich of the *Pittsburgh Post-Gazette*. "We didn't know about all the hate mail that came to him after the championship."

Worsley said it took him ten years before he understood the magnitude of the game. "The older I become, the more I appreciate it," he said. "I can see that it opened up doors for other players and coaches."

Miners forward Nevil "The Shadow" Shed told Simonich, "Racism back in the Sixties was truly right there. Coach Haskins never did let us get a sense of how bad it was. Instead, he focused us on basketball. He was a tenacious, hard-nosed, never-say-die coach, and we played in his image."

As he's grown older, Shed said, he's come to realize the significance of that championship contest. "When an unknown school won with an integrated team, the elite schools had no choice but to take notice."

DID YOU KNOW . . .

- Kentucky players accepted their defeat against Texas Western with grace. Pat Riley, who later became one of the NBA's greatest coaches, sought out the Miners to congratulate them.

- In 1969—three years after losing to Texas Western—Kentucky coach Adolph Rupp recruited his first black player, Tom Payne. By the mid-1970s, black players filled rosters of most southern schools.

- Haskins, who coached at Texas Western/UTEP from 1961 to 1999, always had racially mixed teams. His first group at Texas Western included Nolan Richardson, an African-American who eventually coached Arkansas to a national championship in 1994. Fifteen of the 17 players on the Razorbacks team were black.

"[Texas Western] had finally gotten a lesson across to the SEC, the ACC, and the world: Since that time, no pretender to basketball eminence has ever drawn a color line in its recruiting."
—Basketball historian Neil D. Isaacs

MOVING TARGET

By winning the 1966 championship with an all-black starting team, Texas Western unwittingly stirred racial hatred among bigots that lasted into the next season.

According to the Pittsburgh Post-Gazette, *Coach Don Haskins received a call warning that one of the players on the defending champs would be shot while the team was in Dallas to play Southern Methodist.*

Center Nevil Shed was so edgy by the thought of a sniper that he kept darting away from team huddles. "Nevil, would you keep still," Haskins admonished him.

"Coach," Shed responded, "if I'm a moving target, I'll be harder to hit."

From Fame to Infamy

There have been many years when the NCAA has enjoyed greatness on the court, but 1951 wasn't one of them. In fact, it was the worst ever—because some of its star players were hauled into court in a game-fixing scandal that rocked college basketball.

Less than a year after City College of New York basked in the glory of the NCAA and NIT championships in 1950, it sank in disgrace. And sharing the shame were 1950 NCAA runner-up Bradley, 1948 and 1949 champion Kentucky, Toledo, Manhattan College, New York

University, and Long Island University. In all, 35 active and former players, five fixers, and 14 gamblers were nabbed in schemes that fixed 86 games between 1947 and 1950.

In January 1951, New York District Attorney Frank Hogan indicted Manhattan College players Henry Poppe and Jack Byrnes, and fixers Cornelius Kelleher and brothers Benjamin and Irving Schwartzberg, who were bookmakers with criminal records. All were booked on bribery and conspiracy charges. Hogan claimed that the two players were paid $3,000 to insure that Manhattan lost three games by at least a certain point margin.

But the real shock came a month later when CCNY players Ed Warner, Ed Roman and Alvin Roth—who all played in the NCAA championship game the year before—were arrested on charges of bribery. The following month their teammates, Irwin Dambrot, Norm Mager, Floyd Layne, and Herb Cohen, were arrested. The investigation concluded that three of the five games CCNY lost during the 1950–51 regular season were fixed, and that points were shaved in others. The players were bribed to keep winning margins under the point spread, thereby assuring large profits for fixers who bet big money on the games. The seven CCNY players received suspended sentences, except for Warner, who was sentenced to six months in jail.

The ignominy didn't end there. In the summer of 1951, seven Bradley players who played in the 1950 championship game—Gene Melchiorre, Billy Mann, Bud Grover, Aaron Preece, Mike Chianakas, Fred Schlictman, and Jim Kelly—were charged with taking bribes from gamblers to hold down scores against St. Joseph's and Oregon State. In the fall, Melchiorre, Mann, and Chianakas pleaded guilty to a misdemeanor. Although they faced three years in jail, each received a suspended sentence because of their cooperation. Their four indicted teammates went to trial and were acquitted. (Melchiorre was a top NBA draft pick in 1952, but never played a game because of his involvement in the betting scheme.)

The scandal spread to Long Island University, where six players were convicted, with one serving nine months in prison while the others received suspended sentences. Two former LIU players, who were acting as fixers, were convicted and sentenced to from two to four years in prison. A New York University player was convicted and given a suspended sentence while authorities arrested four Toledo players but eventually dropped the charges. The fixers and gamblers were convicted and received sentences ranging from six months to seven years.

Rumors sprouted that investigators had aimed their

sights at the Kentucky Wildcats. Coach Adolph Rupp claimed his team was untouchable, insisting, "They couldn't reach my boys with a ten-foot pole." He was wrong.

In October 1951, seven months after his team won the NCAA championship for the third time in four years, the hoops world was shaken to its core when Hogan arrested Kentucky stars Ralph Beard and Alex Groza and reserve Dale Barnstable, who all had helped the Wildcats win titles in 1948 and 1949. They were accused of accepting bribes to shave points in some games and to throw the NIT game against Loyola in 1949. That explains why top-ranked Kentucky lost, 67–56, in an upset to 16th-ranked Loyola in the NIT, but then sailed through the NCAA tourney to win the crown.

The trio confessed and were placed on indefinite probation and barred from all sports for three years. Because Beard and Groza were playing in the NBA at the time of their convictions, NBA commissioner Maurice Podoloff banned them for life.

Toward the end of the investigation, Bill Spivey, Kentucky's All-American center and leading player on the 1951 NCAA championship squad, was accused by teammates of point shaving. Even though he denied it, the university kicked him off the team. In 1953, Hogan indicted Spivey for perjury, but he was never convicted.

Nevertheless, the NBA banned him from ever playing in the league.

Meanwhile, the NCAA slapped the prestigious Kentucky basketball program with its harshest penalty of the scandal. It suspended the team's entire 1952–53 season.

Presiding judge Saul Streit blasted Rupp, calling the UK basketball program "the acme of commercialism and overemphasis." He blamed Rupp for creating a harmful atmosphere for the student athletes, adding that the coach "failed in his duty to observe the amateur rules, to build character, and to protect the morals and health of his charges." Rupp vigorously denied the criticism and claimed he knew nothing about the fixed games. But the scandal stained his reputation anyway.

As for CCNY, the Board of Higher Education uncovered another sneaky scheme. The high school records of 14 players had been changed to make them eligible for admission to the school. Coach Nat Holman was suspended, but he won his job back on an appeal. The board banned the team from playing at Madison Square Garden—the mecca of college basketball at that time—and ordered the school to de-emphasize its hoops program. City College never again returned to hoops prominence. Today the Beavers compete in the NCAA Division III's City University of

New York Athletic Conference—far removed from the glory days when the team became the first and only school to ever win the NIT and NCAA titles in the same year.

DID YOU KNOW . . .

- *Newsday* listed the scandal as the worst event in New York sports history. ESPN.com ranked it second only to the 1919 Chicago Black Sox on its list of all-time worst sports scandals.

"For these guys to sell out their school and themselves and their careers for eight hundred dollars, for a thousand dollars, for fifteen hundred dollars was just such an emotional blow. You never really recover from something like that. It is a wound in your psyche that lasts all your life… It is a little bit of a burden for all of us to carry who were in school at the time."

—Sportswriter Maury Allen, CCNY class of '53

A Team Scorned

Even though his team finished the regular 1953–54 season with a perfect 25-0 record, Kentucky coach Adolph Rupp turned down an invitation to the Big Dance.

When the NCAA banned the team from playing any games throughout the previous season because of the game-fixing scandal, the players stayed together and practiced with one goal in mind: to come back the following year and win the national championship. Even though UK's top three stars had graduated, they chose to delay their pro careers so they could use up their remaining year of eligibility.

At the beginning of the 1953–54 season, Rupp reportedly boasted, "We have a new scoreboard that can register beyond 100 points, so we'll score half for the season we missed and half for this season." (The Wildcats reached beyond the century mark three times at home that year.)

Playing with a vengeance, Kentucky roared through the season undefeated, whipping its opponents by an average margin of 27 points. But there was a complication. The team's three biggest stars—Cliff Hagan, Frank Ramsey, and Lou Tsioropoulos—were finishing their basketball eligibility as graduate students. According to the rules at the time, they were eligible to play in the regular season but not in the NCAA Tournament.

Knowing the team would get an invitation to the tournament, the school asked the NCAA earlier in the year to waive the rule because it was never intended to cover UK's extraordinary situation in which the graduate players didn't have the opportunity to compete as seniors. Despite the early appeal, the NCAA didn't respond until Kentucky won the SEC championship. Unfortunately for the Wildcats, the NCAA denied the appeal, which meant the three players weren't eligible for the tournament.

The rest of the team voted to play in the tourney anyway, but Rupp was so furious at the NCAA that he refused the invitation. Directing his ire at Walter Byers, head of the NCAA, Rupp told reporters, "I'll not retire until the man who said Kentucky can't play . . . hands me the national championship trophy." Rupp would have to wait until 1958.

That was little satisfaction to the undefeated 1953–54 squad, especially since earlier in the year Kentucky had drubbed eventual champion La Salle, 73–60. As far as the Wildcats were concerned, Kentucky was the best team in the land.

Tarnished Tournament

The 1971 NCAA Tournament was tarnished more than any other because two players who led their teams to the Final Four were professionals—a secret that wasn't exposed until weeks later. As a result, for the first and only time, the NCAA vacated the names of the second- and third-place teams and the winner of the Most Outstanding

Player award.

The scandal rubbed some of the luster off the fourth consecutive title won by the UCLA Bruins, who had nothing to do with the shame.

Even before the tournament began, rumors floated around that All-Americans Howard Porter of Villanova and Jim McDaniels of Western Kentucky had signed pro contracts with the American Basketball Association. Doing so would have rendered the two stars ineligible to play college basketball. Each denied turning pro. However, there was enough suspicion to cause the NCAA to demand that the two sign affidavits claiming they still were amateurs. When they complied, the NCAA allowed them to compete.

The two players led their teams to the semifinals, where Villanova squeaked past Western Kentucky, 92–89, in double overtime. McDaniels was the high scorer for the Hilltoppers, while Porter scored 22 points and had 16 rebounds.

In the championship game, which UCLA won, 68–62, Porter pumped in 25 points and grabbed eight boards, and was named the tournament's Most Outstanding Player. Meanwhile, McDaniels sparked his team to a 77–75 victory over Kansas in a battle for third place. Both players made the all-tournament team.

But then, the ABA's Pittsburgh Condors admitted they had signed Porter before the Final Four. And it was discovered that the Utah Stars had McDaniels under contract since before the tournament.

When the truth was revealed, the NCAA stripped Villanova and Western Kentucky of their respective second- and third-place finishes. Porter's award was rescinded and his name and McDaniels's name were deleted from the all-tournament team.

Porter's ABA contract was voided, but he went on to play in the NBA for seven seasons, averaging 9.2 points and 4.1 rebounds per game while McDaniels played one year in the ABA and four years in the NBA, averaging 5.1 points and 4.2 rebounds per game.

According to Porter's teammate, Ed Hastings, the shame and guilt that Porter felt over the scandal weighed heavily upon him for a long time. Porter's life spiraled out of control, fueled by divorce, bankruptcy, cocaine addiction, and jail time. "I took a ride with the devil," he said years later. After hitting rock bottom, Porter went through a treatment program and cleaned himself up to become a counselor.

In 1996 he returned to Villanova for the first time to see his number retired and to celebrate the 25th anniversary of the team's 1971 tournament run. Writing in

Villanova Magazine, Hastings said, "Everyone was excited to see one another, but most especially Howard. Most of us had not seen him in 20 years or so. He assumed incorrectly that he would be resented, not only by Villanovans in general, but also by his teammates. This was completely untrue about his teammates. As a team, we always supported Howard and took his side. We knew that we would never have achieved what we did without him and we knew in our hearts that it would have been exceedingly difficult for any of us to have done anything differently than he did, given our maturity levels, the tough circumstances and the offered money."

The Not-so-Fab Five

The NCAA Tournament had never seen anything like them. Five trash-talking, high-styling freshmen with awesome talent had strutted their way to the 1992 championship game. And then, as sophomores, they did it again.

They drew record television audiences, set fashion trends, and ignited a licensing and merchandising boom in college sports.

Michigan Wolverines Chris Webber, Juwan Howard, Jalen Rose, Ray Jackson, and Jimmy King—nicknamed the Fab Five—brought fame to their school.

And one of them brought shame—so much so that the NCAA vacated Michigan's participation in the 1992 and 1993 championship games.

When they burst on the college scene, the Fab Five were the hip-hop artists of hoops. They sported shaved heads and wore baggy shorts. They bumped chests and slapped hands. They talked smack to opponents and beat them, too, with 56 victories in two years.

They attracted attention wherever they played. The 1992 final—a 71–51 loss to Duke—remains the most-watched game in college basketball history, with 20.9 million homes tuned to the telecast. The 1993 final—a 77–71 defeat to North Carolina—is the second-most-watched game ever, viewed in almost 20.7 million homes.

They were treated like rock stars. "We were almost compared to somebody like the Beatles," Howard told *USA Today* reporter Steve Wieberg in 2002. "We used to go on the road, and there'd be fans lined up outside our hotel wanting our autographs. There'd be people on the campus selling T-shirts with our names on them, with our faces on them."

The Fab Five made the Michigan brand red-hot, and the school cashed in. Annual athletic royalties more than tripled from $2 million in the pre-Fab year of 1990–91 to a peak of $6.2 million in 1993–94. Other schools took notice and boosted their own efforts at marketing their teams, raking in tens of millions of dollars.

But the Fab Five never won a conference or a national title. Webber left for the NBA after his sophomore year; Rose and Howard followed after their junior year.

And then came the scandal.

An investigation revealed that now-deceased Michigan booster Ed Martin, who had unlimited access to the players, gave hundreds of thousands of dollars to former Wolverines while they were in high school and college. One of the players was Chris Webber. Martin pleaded guilty in 2002 to conspiracy to launder money, and confessed he lent $616,000 to Webber and players Maurice Taylor, Robert Traylor, and Louis Bullock. Rose later admitted to receiving "pocket money" from Martin.

Martin said he gave Webber $280,000 from 1988 to 1993—a charge Webber denied. Webber was indicted on perjury charges stemming from his appearance in a grand jury investigating the Martin affair. The player eventually pleaded guilty to criminal contempt and was fined $100,000 and ordered to complete 300 hours of community service.

Michigan officials hoped the NCAA would accept its self-imposed sanctions. They included the removal from Crisler Arena of four banners commemorating the

Wolverines' high finishes in NCAA tournaments and any pictures, words, or records in printed materials involving Webber and the other players named in the scandal; forfeits of 112 regular-season and tournament victories from five seasons, plus its victory in the 1992 NCAA semifinals; and the return of $450,000 to the NCAA from tainted post-season appearances.

The NCAA said that wasn't enough punishment. In 2003, the Wolverines were barred from the next post-season and put on $3\frac{1}{2}$ years' probation. The team also lost one of its 13 annual scholarships for four years, and had its championship game appearances in 1992 and 1993 vacated.

"This is one of the most egregious violations of NCAA laws in the history of the organization," Thomas Yeager, NCAA Committee on Infractions chairman, said at the time. "The reputation of the university, the student-athletes and the coach as a result of the basketball team's accomplishments from 1992 through 1998 were a sham."

The Game that Almost Wasn't

The 1981 championship game at the Spectrum in Philadelphia was arguably the most controversial of all—simply because it was played as scheduled.

Just six hours earlier on March 30, President Ronald

Reagan was seriously wounded in an assassination attempt. Lone gunman John Hinckley had opened fire at close range as the president was leaving a Washington hotel following a speech he had given. The shooter squeezed off at least five rounds, also wounding White House Press Secretary James Brady in the head, a Secret Service man, and a Washington policeman before the cops pushed the gunman to the ground.

The attempted murder shocked many Americans who still had vivid memories of the assassination of President John F. Kennedy in 1963. Reagan, who had been shot in the chest, was rushed into emergency surgery.

Officials for the Academy Awards show, slated for broadcast that night, quickly announced they were postponing the ceremony for 24 hours. But the NCAA brass weren't willing to do the same thing. In fact, they gave the go-ahead for LSU and Virginia to play in the consolation game scheduled for 5 p.m.

The championship game between Indiana and North Carolina was supposed to tip off at 8:23 p.m. on NBC. But as time drew near, there was no word on the game's status from the NCAA Division I Basketball Committee members who had gathered at the Spectrum. It was their call to make. The clock struck 7 p.m., and then 7:30.

The committee, headed by Big Ten commissioner

Wayne Duke, was waiting for a report from the hospital on the president's condition before deciding the game's fate.

Finally, Dr. Dennis O'Leary, dean of clinical affairs at George Washington University Hospital, announced that surgery on the president had been successful and he was out of danger. The committee then gave the okay to play. At 8:15 p.m., NBC News ended its live coverage from the capital of the assassination attempt, and the network switched to basketball.

Duke told reporters that, if the medical report had been anything less than positive, the game would have been postponed. And he insisted that the television people were not involved. "I have no second thoughts," he declared. Maybe not, but he and NBC were bashed in the press—and even on the air by the network's own sports-casters.

Said Bryant Gumbel, who was host of NBC's pre-game show, "It makes the people covering this game look like this is all we care about. My personal opinion is that they shouldn't play. There is a time to play and a time not to play. If the Academy Awards can be pushed back, so can the NCAA finals. ABC and CBS are on the air [reporting on the assassination attempt], and we're playing games. It doesn't look good for us. It makes us look like callous boobs."

Play-by-play announcer Dick Enberg told the audience, "We'd hoped they would postpone the game 24 hours."

Added garrulous analyst Al McGuire, "I want the people to know that I'm here because this is my job. I really don't think my saloon style fits in this kind of atmosphere. I would have preferred not to be on the air tonight."

The players, who had been in their locker rooms waiting and wondering if there would be a game, wanted to play. And the fans at the Spectrum wanted to see a game. While President Reagan lay in intensive care, Indiana, sparked by Isiah Thomas's 23 points, battered North Carolina, 63–50.

DID YOU KNOW . . .
• When Virginia defeated Louisiana State 78–74, it was the last time that Final Four losers would ever have to play for third place in the NCAA Tournament.

"Even now, it is hard to believe that this completely homegrown gang of kids who started as virtually 'nothing' have come upon everything. But if you look back on their untiring labors, their sacrifices and, above all else, their determination to overcome all obstacles on the road to success, then it shouldn't be such a surprise."

—The *San Francisco Examiner's* Bob Brachman on the 1955 national champion University of San Francisco Dons

SPECIAL TEAMS

Dunking the Dunkers

The North Carolina State Wolfpack pulled off one of the title game's biggest surprises in 1983 when the team shot down the high-flying, rim-rattling dunkers from Houston, 54–52.

Ironically, the Cougars—nicknamed Phi Slamma Jamma because of their penchant for dunking the ball— lost the game on, of all things, a dunk.

Anybody who knew anything about college basketball figured the championship game would be a laugher. Houston seemed unbeatable. Possessing a lofty 31-2 record and a No. 1 national ranking to go with its No. 1 seed, the Cougars featured Akeem "The Dream" Olajuwon and Clyde "The Glide" Drexler—both of whom would be

named years later to the NBA's Top 50 of All-Time. The
Cougars, winners of 26 straight, blitzed through the tourney, including winning a jamfest against No. 2 Louisville,
94–81, in the semifinals. They scored 58 second-half
points, 22 from dunks.

The No. 6 seed Wolfpack, on the other hand, chugged
into the finals with a 25-10 mark—not bad for a team
near the bottom of the top 25 rankings, but unheard of for
one vying for the championship. In fact, up until then, no
team had won the title with so many losses. N.C. State
didn't inspire much fear, especially after it needed double
overtime to beat No. 11 seed Pepperdine, 69–67, in the
opening round and, among its other tourney victories,
squeaked past UNLV and Virginia, each by a single point.

Wrote Joe Henderson of the *Tampa* (Florida) *Tribune*
before the game, "Blindfold? Cigarette? Last Words?
Sayonara, N.C. State. There'll be no reprieve. The noose
drops at 9:12 p.m. (starting time)."

The Wolfpack's quotable, laugh-a-minute Coach Jim
Valvano played up the underdog role. Claiming to be so
awed by Houston's running and leaping juggernaut, the
coach told the press, "If we get the opening tip, we may
not take a shot until Tuesday morning." (There was no
shot clock back then.) When reports surfaced that his
players were out past curfew, Valvano joked, "I want every-

body to know I had a bed check last night and all the beds were there."

The truth was that Valvano was as smart as he was funny, and he came up with a game plan that put Phi Slamma Jamma on notice that they were in for the fight of their lives. Playing tough defense and a slow-down tempo, the Wolfpack frustrated Houston and went into halftime at University Arena in Albuquerque with a 33–25 lead.

But the Cougars roared to life at the start of the second half and went on a 17–2 binge to surge ahead, 42–35. Just when it seemed that N.C. State was on the ropes, Houston coach Guy Lewis ordered his team to slow it down and spread the offense, hoping to draw the Wolfpack out of their zone defense. The strategy backfired, and N.C. State crept back into the game, tying it, 52–52, with two minutes left.

On Valvano's instructions, Cougars freshman guard Alvin Franklin was fouled with 1:08 remaining. He missed the front end of a one-and-one—just as the coach had figured. After getting the rebound, the Wolfpack held the ball for the final shot, making 16 passes. But with less than ten seconds left, a pass from Thurl Bailey to Dereck Whittenburg was slapped away. In the scramble, Whittenburg grabbed the ball and heaved a desperation shot from about 35 feet away. It was an air ball.

But the Wolfpack's 6-foot-7 sophomore, Lorenzo Charles, had slipped down the lane uncontested because Olajuwon had taken a step upcourt following Bailey's contested pass. As a result, Charles was perfectly positioned in front of the basket. He caught the ball in midair and slammed it through the net. One second later, it was over.

As fans and players stormed the court, Charles stood frozen under the basket as if trying to comprehend the magnitude of his dunk. Bailey fell to the floor sobbing with happiness while teammate Sidney Lowe raced into the stands to hug his mother. Valvano, his arms outstretched, darted willy-nilly on the floor in search of someone, anyone, to embrace.

Against all odds, N.C. State had toppled Houston for the national title.

"If we played them 20 times, I still don't think they'd win but that one game," said Clyde Drexler. "So it had to be destiny."

DID YOU KNOW . . .

• Jim Valvano coached the championship game while suffering from a terrible case of the flu and a 104-degree fever. Trainer Jim Rehbock had to give Valvano intravenous fluids before the team left the hotel for the arena. As soon as Valvano finished talking with the press after the game, team doctors ordered him to bed. "Imagine that," Rehbock said. "He wins the national championship, it's the biggest night of his life, and he has to head back to the hotel and go to bed. But he didn't even fight it. That will tell you how sick he was."

• The Wolfpack should have been called the Cardiac Kids. They won four of their six tournament games by two points or less, including a double-overtime.

"It was bigger than a basketball game. I remember some of the letters we got, the effect we had on people's lives. They'd say watching us play inspired them to achieve more, to be better people. It taught a lesson about chasing your dreams."

—North Carolina State player Thurl Bailey, reflecting years later on his team's dramatic 54–52 upset of Houston for the 1983 national championship

Near Perfection

In a classic stunner, unheralded Villanova dethroned top-ranked defending champion Georgetown to claim the 1985 prize in a rather unusual way.

The Wildcats won it all even though they set a Final Four record for the fewest field goals attempted—just 28. However, they also set a Final Four record for highest field goal percentage—a sizzling 78.6 on 22 of 28 shooting. And they did it against the nation's toughest defense, which had held opponents to under 40 percent shooting.

It didn't seem possible that Villanova had a chance against mighty Georgetown because on paper it looked like a slaughter in the making. The Hoyas were 35-2; the Wildcats were 24-10. Georgetown was led by three future NBA stars—All-American center Patrick Ewing, Reggie Williams, and David Wingate; Villanova had one NBA prospect, Ed Pinckney. The Hoyas were making their fourth Final Four appearance in six years; the Wildcats previously had never made it past the Elite Eight. Georgetown was ranked at the top of the national polls and was a No. 1 seed; Villanova hadn't been ranked in the top 20 all year and was seeded eighth in the tourney. The Hoyas had beaten the Wildcats twice during the regular season.

What a mismatch! Or so it seemed. But, as they say,

that's why you play the game.

Villanova remained poised and patient, playing stingy defense and working the ball around the perimeter for a good shot. To most everyone's surprise, the Wildcats held a slim 29–28 lead at intermission.

Despite Georgetown's intense pressure, Villanova played nearly flawlessly in the second half, making nine of ten shots. After the lead changed hands nine times, the Wildcats jumped in front with 2:36 left and held on for the startling win. Pinckney, who scored 16 points and had six rebounds, held Ewing to 14 points and five boards. The victors made 22 of 27 free throws to the losers' six of eight.

The disappointed Hoyas showed their class at the trophy presentation immediately after the game. As the Wildcats mounted the victory stand, the Georgetown players stood and applauded them. "Any time you shoot that percentage, you deserve the praise," said Georgetown coach John Thompson. "You couldn't get much better."

DID YOU KNOW . . .

- Villanova also holds the mark by being the lowest seed (8th) ever to win the championship since the tournament began seeding in 1979.

THE FIDDLIN' FIVE

At the beginning of the 1957–58 season, Kentucky coach Adolph Rupp told the press he didn't think he had a championship caliber team, adding, "They might be pretty good barnyard fiddlers, but we have a Carnegie Hall schedule. And it will take violinists to play that competition." Everyone then started calling the team the Fiddlin' Five.

Despite a 19-6 regular season—the worst in school history since 1941—the Wildcats won the national championship by defeating Seattle, 84–72.

Said Rupp, "They weren't the greatest basketball players in the world. All they could do was win."

It's Payback Time

Perhaps no Final Four game had more of a revenge factor than the 1968 clash between the UCLA Bruins and Houston Cougars.

The year before, the undefeated Bruins met the seventh-ranked Cougars in the semifinals in Louisville, featuring a match-up of dominating players—UCLA center Lew Alcindor (now known as Kareem Abdul-Jabbar) and Houston forward Elvin "The Big E" Hayes. Although Hayes pumped in 25 points and grabbed 24 boards to Alcindor's 19 points and 20 rebounds, the Bruins won going away, 73–58, and then claimed the title the next day against Dayton.

Nine months later, on January 20, 1968, the second-ranked Cougars sought to avenge that loss when they took on the top-ranked Bruins in the mammoth Houston Astrodome in front of 52,693 fans. It was the largest crowd ever to see a basketball game in the United States up to that time. More than 150 television stations in 49 states broadcast the game to millions of households.

Both teams were undefeated, although UCLA was on a 47-game winning streak. In the tense, back-and-forth contest, Hayes came up really big—39 points (including the winning two free throws), 15 rebounds, eight blocked shots—and carried his team to a 71–69 triumph. It was the first time Alcindor (15 points, 12 rebounds) had been on a losing team since he had joined the varsity the previous year.

The following week, a *Sports Illustrated* cover showed Hayes shooting a jumper over Alcindor. The photo galled Alcindor; the defeat haunted him. He taped the cover to his locker to remind him every day of that stinging loss, hoping, like the rest of the Bruins, for a chance at a payback during the NCAA Tournament.

He and his teammates got their wish two months later when UCLA—its loss to the Cougars its only blemish on an otherwise perfect record—met undefeated Houston in the national semifinals, this time at the Los Angeles Memorial Sports Arena. Coach John Wooden didn't need to motivate his players. They wanted to prove they were the better team. And, boy, did they.

The Bruins broke up a tight game with a 17–5 run that grew to a stunning 22-point halftime lead. Playing virtually flawless basketball, UCLA built an astonishing 44-point margin before Wooden put in his subs as the Bruins crushed the Cougars, 101–69. Alcindor matched two teammates for scoring honors with 19. As for Hayes, he managed a meager ten points and was so mortified that he watched the final minutes of the game on the bench with a towel over his head.

"We haven't really said anything publicly, but we're a vindictive team," UCLA guard Mike Warren told the press afterwards. "We've been looking forward to this game for a long time."

The battle for the title the next night against North Carolina was almost an afterthought. The Bruins thrashed the Tar Heels, 78–55, in what was then the biggest rout in NCAA championship game history.

When Lowly Seeds Sprout

Sometimes Cinderella gets to dance past midnight at the NCAA ball.

Sometimes a lowly seeded team, ignored by all but a few, unexpectedly dazzles everyone by winning games it shouldn't be winning as it spins and twirls its way through the brackets.

In 1986, No. 11 seed Louisiana State became the lowest seeded team ever to make it as far as the Final Four—a feat duplicated in 2006 by George Mason University.

Unranked LSU was lucky just to get an invitation to the Big Dance after dropping 11 of its last 19 regular season games and getting bounced out of the SEC Tournament in the second round. Yet the 22-11 Tigers overcame injuries, a chicken pox epidemic, and academic ineligibilities throughout the season to embark on one of the most improbable runs of any team in NCAA Tournament history.

In the opening round, they dismantled the sixth-seeded Purdue Boilermakers, 94–87, in a double- overtime thriller in front of a hometown crowd of 13,749 at the Maravich Assembly Center in Baton Rouge. LSU guard Anthony Wilson, who scored a career-best 25 points, went to the line on each of the Tigers's final four possessions in overtime, sinking seven of eight free throws.

Two days later, Wilson was the hero again, this time against No. 3 seed Memphis State (now University of Memphis). A veteran 28-5 team, it had been to the Final

Four the year before and had three seniors who would end up in the NBA. Memphis State built a 10-point lead over LSU in the second half but couldn't hold it. With the score tied 81–81 and only five ticks left on the clock, a missed shot by LSU's Don Redden triggered a mad scramble for the rebound. Wilson scooped up the loose ball and shot an eight-foot jumper. It kissed off the glass, bounced twice on the rim and dropped through the hoop at the buzzer for an 83–81 victory.

"It was the greatest feeling I've ever had since I've competed in sports," said Wilson. "I used to dream about making a shot like that when I was a kid."

Pandemonium broke out in the sold-out crowd as Wilson's teammates rushed to the floor to mob him. When he emerged from the pile of players, Coach Dale Brown gave him a big hug. "It was the first time in my life I've ever been out of breath," Brown said.

After enjoying the home-crowd advantage the last two games, LSU faced No. 2 seed, sixth-ranked Georgia Tech (27-6) at the Omni in Atlanta, just six blocks from the Yellow Jackets's campus.

But if the Tigers were intimidated, they didn't show it. Relying on a suffocating press that forced 17 turnovers and stellar ball-handling, LSU silenced the raucous Tech fans by swatting the Yellow Jackets, 70–64.

Now in the Elite Eight, the Tigers needed to beat the No. 1 seed Kentucky Wildcats (32-3) to become the first No. 11 seed ever to reach the Final Four. This would be no easy task. LSU had lost 11 of its last 15 meetings with Kentucky, including three earlier in the season. In addition, the Wildcats had won 14 straight games and 21 in a row over SEC opponents.

But Coach Brown felt good about his team's chances. He told his players before the game that he had the same feeling he had when LSU made it to the Final Four five years earlier as a No. 1 seed. Also, he told them, he heard the tune, "You Gotta Have Heart," on the radio. "We can't beat this team today without it."

The Tigers were loose. "If the pressure is on anybody, it's on Kentucky," said LSU forward Don Redden before the game. "They're the No. 1 seed and they're supposed to get to the Final Four. We're the Cinderella team."

LSU scored on eight of its final ten possessions for a surprising 59–57 victory. The Tigers were now one of only four teams left standing—and the only squad among the quartet that wasn't ranked. They were with some impressive company at the Reunion Arena in Dallas—Duke, Kansas and their next opponent, No. 2 seed Louisville (30-7).

For the first 20 minutes against the Cardinals, the

Cinderella team was having a ball, waltzing out to a 44–36 halftime lead. But then, after Louisville squeezed them with a full-court press that sparked a 17–1 run, the clock struck midnight for the Tigers. They lost, 88–77, to Louisville, who then beat Duke, 72–69, for the national championship.

"I thought we played as hard as we possibly could," said Brown. "We could not expect more out of this team. They gave it everything they had the entire tournament, and I can't be more proud of what we did this season. We earned our way here. We had the hardest road to the Final Four, and we got here through a democratic system of playing games. We're an example of what makes America great."

* * *

After getting knocked out of the Colonial Athletic Association tournament, the George Mason Patriots had to hold their breath when the 2006 NCAA Tournament brackets were announced. Then, they had to hold their tongues when sportswriters and fans questioned why a squad from the lightly-regarded CAA would get an at-large berth while teams from the more respected Big East and Atlantic Coast Conference were spurned.

Well, the Patriots showed them why. GMU became only the second No. 11 seed ever to make it all the way to the Final Four.

In the opening round in Dayton, Ohio, the Patriots (23-7), who had never won an NCAA Tournament game, squared off against No. 6 seed Michigan State (22-11), which had been to the Final Four four times in the past seven years.

Before the opening tip, GMU coach Jim Larranaga gave his green-uniformed team something to think about. Recalled the coach, "The last comment I made to them was, 'What color is kryptonite?' They said, 'Green.' I said, 'Look at your jerseys. You have everything you need to win this game.'"

He was right. The underdogs used hot shooting, a balanced attack, a late 10–0 run, and unexpected rebounding superiority (40–24) to upset the Spartans, 75–65.

Next, the suburban commuter school from Fairfax, Virginia, took on defending champion North Carolina (23-7), a No. 3 seed. The Patriots shrugged off a 16–2 Tar Heel run at the start of the game and scrambled to cut the deficit to 27–20 at the half. In the locker room, Larranaga calmly delivered a lecture. "It was like a teacher talking to his students about an upcoming test," he recalled. "I said to them, 'You're so well-prepared for this, and you've done it so consistently for such a long time, there is no reason we shouldn't do it again.'"

George Mason came out in the second half and forced six turnovers in North Carolina's first seven possessions. The Patriots hit 10 of their first 13 shots and spurted into the lead. Clamping down on defense, they held the Tar Heels 20 points below their average and won in another upset, 65–60.

And just like that the Patriots became America's darlings. Every sports section in the country featured stories about the team, players and coach. "I told our players, 'If you can't have fun and enjoy the excitement surrounding our program, you can't get excited about anything,'" said Larranaga.

In its Sweet Sixteen game against No. 7 seed Wichita State (26-8), GMU jumped out to a 9–0 lead and led by as many as 19. Folarin Campbell had 16 points to pace a balanced attack that hit eight of 16 three-pointers. Once again, the Patriots defense was tough, limiting the Shockers to less than 32 percent shooting in a 63–55 triumph.

"It's not supposed to happen, but we're making it happen," said GMU guard Tony Skinn of his team's appearance in the Elite Eight, where they faced tournament favorite, No. 1 seed Connecticut (30-3).

When word got out that the Huskies didn't know anything about George Mason or its conference, the CAA, the Patriots took it as a sign of disrespect. Larranaga told his players that the CAA stood for the Connecticut Assassins Association, and then used his fingers as six-shooters.

The Patriots blazed away and the Huskies fired back. Trailing by nine early in the second half, George Mason rallied against the much taller, more experienced UConn and took a late four-point lead. But it slipped away when the Huskies's Denham Brown scored a layup to tie the game at the end of regulation.

Displaying remarkable poise, the Patriots regrouped and hit five of six shots in overtime for a stunning 86–84 upset victory. They had matched LSU's run in 1986 and were now in the prestigious Final Four. They became the biggest outsider—a team with no basketball tradition, superstar player, or membership in a major conference—to make it this far since Ivy League school Penn did it in 1979.

"It shows [that you should] never stop dreaming no matter how old you are," said guard Lamar Butler.

By now, George Mason's warm-and-fuzzy fairy tale had captured the hearts of sports fans everywhere. TV appearances, press interviews and autograph sessions filled their days between class and practice. Butler said he received two marriage proposals at a school pep rally. A coed carried a sign that said, "Lamar Butler, will you marry me?" Next to her was another young woman with a sign that said, "No. Marry me."

While the other Final Four teams kept their practices closed, Larranaga opened his up to 400 members of the press. At the end of practice, his team played unity-ball—a baseball game played with a paper ball covered in tape and a foam-and-plastic bat. "The whole idea is to stay upbeat, positive, totally committed to what we want to do and what we want to accomplish, but just do it in a relaxed atmosphere," the coach explained.

All the hoopla was getting under the skin of GMU's next opponent, the No. 3 seed Florida Gators (31-6). "It's time to kiss Cinderella and send her home," groused Florida forward Corey Brewer. And that's just what the Gators did—except without the kissing.

Florida drilled 12 of 25 three-pointers to GMU's 2 of 11 and dramatically out-rebounded the shorter Patriots, 40–27, as the Gators cruised to a 73-58 win, ending the most unlikely run in 20 years. (Florida then crushed UCLA, 73–57, for the title.)

"We've done something tremendous for college basketball, for the teams that watched us play, just to show them that all you need is a chance," said Tony Skinn after

George Mason's disappointing loss.

Added Butler, "We changed the face of college basketball."

DID YOU KNOW . . .

• George Mason was one of only three teams since 1981 to enter without a tournament win in its school history and still reach the Final Four. Georgia did it in 1983 and Virginia gained that distinction in 1981—when its assistant coach was none other than Jim Larranaga.

Saints Alive!

Siena College just might have been the oddest team ever to participate in the NCAA Tournament.

It played the entire 1988–89 regular season without a team name. And it played its last nine games prior to the tourney without any fans in the stands. It wasn't that the team was bad. Quite the contrary. It entered the Big Dance with an impressive 24-4 record. What set this team apart from all others was that it got caught in a perfect storm of unexpected events.

At the beginning of the season, officials of the tiny Catholic school in Loudonville, New York, decided that the team name, the Indians, was insensitive to Native Americans and banned its use. Rather than rush into picking any old name, the school asked students and fans for suggestions—a process that took many months. So the Siena basketball team played without a name.

Then in early February, the campus was struck by a measles outbreak. Because measles is quite contagious, medical authorities were concerned that students who were carrying the disease might spread it if they were allowed to attend basketball games. So quarantine signs were posted at the basketball arena, which was now off limits to spectators. While fans, pep bands, and cheerleaders remained home, Siena's no-names played their next nine games in front of nobody except reporters, photographers and team and school officials.

During the quarantine period, Siena's sophomore sensation, Marc Brown, was asked what it was like to play to the sounds of silence. "At first it was different, new," he told the press. "But now, it's starting to wear on me. I'm a little flashy; I like to make a nice pass and hear the crowd cheer. But no one cheers."

When a subsequent measles outbreak hit the University of Hartford, officials extended the ban to the eight-team North Atlantic Conference Tournament, which would determine who went to the NCAA Tournament. Although players on all the NAC teams had been vaccinated, two, including one from Siena, contracted the disease.

Some of the teams seemed a little spooked by playing in the virtually empty 15,414-seat Hartford Civic Center. But the nameless team from Siena felt right at home and won the conference title, 68–67, over Boston University on a last-second basket by Steve McCoy.

And then life changed dramatically for Siena. The team got a new name, which was announced to the world on ESPN. After considering 150 suggestions, the school settled on the Saints. (It rejected a late quarantine-inspired entry, the Ravin' Rash.)

The team earned its first invitation ever to the Big Dance, which meant it would finally play in front of a crowd for its opening round game in Greensboro, North Carolina, where there was no measles quarantine. Siena fans, thrilled at the opportunity to see their team play in person for the first time in six weeks, crammed in a caravan of 14 buses and hundreds of cars for the long trek to the Tar Heel state.

Conventional wisdom said it would be a short visit because the Saints were seeded 14th and going against the No. 3 seed Stanford Cardinal, (who also had ditched the name Indians out of cultural respect, back in 1972). Even though Stanford was expected to win easily and play a second-round game two days later, Siena coach Mike Deane brought two suits. "It would have been a bad omen to bring only one," he said. His wife came with only enough clothes for one game. She would need to buy more.

Siena fans showed up wearing T-shirts that read, "Siena Saints 98.6, Measles 0" and cheered their hearts out before the game even started. They created such a scene that one of the players turned to his teammates and said, "I feel like one of the Beatles."

With a new name and terrific fan support, Siena walked onto the court with confidence. In a pre-game interview, sophomore Tom Huerter told a national TV audience that the Saints "liked the match-up we have with Stanford because they won't be able to overwhelm us athletically."

He was right, sort of. Siena built a 16-point lead only to watch Stanford mount a furious late-game rally that tied the score. But then Marc Brown, the high scorer with 32 points, coolly sank two free throws with three seconds left to carry his team to a startling 80–78 upset victory.

Siena lost in the next round to Minnesota, 80–67, but at least the tiny school had made a name for itself in more ways than one.

Stomping the Top Seeds

Although the Arizona Wildcats seemed an unlikely team to win the 1997 championship, they certainly were no fluke. They were the first team in NCAA history to knock off three No. 1 seeds on its way to the title.

The Wildcats, who finished fifth in the Pacific-10 Conference, entered the tournament as a No. 4 seed with a 19-9 record. In the opening round, they trailed South Alabama by ten with less than four minutes to play before rallying for a 65–57 victory. Next, they edged College of Charleston, 73–69.

Arizona then pulled off an upset, staggering the nation's top-ranked team, No. 1 seed Kansas, 85–82. After slipping past Providence, 96–92, in overtime, the Wildcats beat No. 1 seed North Carolina, 66–58. They were still the underdogs when they clawed their way to the title with another overtime triumph, this one over their third top-seeded team, Kentucky, 84–79.

Arizona became the only champion to win all six of its playoff contests by single-digit margins since 1950 when only eight teams were in the tournament and three victories earned a title.

By the way, the six victories in the tournament were Arizona's longest winning streak of the season.

"I still have a hard time believing this has really happened."
—Coach Lute Olson after his Arizona Wildcats beat the Kentucky
Wildcats, 84–79, in the 1997 title game

Bald Eagles

For the 2006 tournament, the Boston College Eagles
decided they needed a Mr. Clean look. So all but one
shaved their heads before their opening round game.

It was BC guard Louis Hinnant's idea. Although he
made it in jest, the notion was adopted by the players, who
submitted their heads to the razor. But not everyone was
thrilled—including Hinnant.

"I really love my hair," he told reporters, "but I had to
do it. The rest of the team did it, and I can't let my teammates down."

The only one who backed out was Jared Dudley, the
team's dreadlocked forward. He argued that cutting his
hair would mess up his game. "Him putting so many years
into grooming that style, I don't think he's going to cut it,"
said Hinnant.

The rest of the team didn't get down on Dudley for his
hairy attitude, especially since he scored 43 points in BC's
first two tournament victories. Villanova then shot down
the Eagles, 60–59 in overtime.

Like Fathers, Like Sons

The 2005–06 Florida Gators were the first championship team to have three starters who are the sons of professional athletes.

Joakim Noah, Al Horford, and Taurean Green come from sporting stock.

Noah is the son of Yannick Noah, the 1983 French Open tennis champion, and Cecilia Rhode, second runner-up in the 1978 Miss Universe pageant and former Miss Sweden. Horford's father, Tito Horford, played center for the Washington Bullets in 1988–90 and Milwaukee Bucks in 1993–94 in between stints in France, Italy, and Brazil. Green's father, Sidney Green, was a forward for five NBA teams from 1983 to 1993.

In the Gators's 73–57 rout of the UCLA Bruins for the 2006 championship, the sons did their fathers proud. Playing center and forward, Noah was named the tournament's Most Outstanding Player after scoring 16 points, swiping nine rebounds, and blocking a title-game record six shots. Horford, a forward, tallied 14 points and seven boards while Green, a guard, had a game-high eight assists.

Florida coach Billy Donovan said the three players never felt a sense of entitlement because their dads were professional athletes.

Speaking to Mark Schlabach of the *Washington Post*,

Donovan said, "I think Yannick Noah lining up and playing tennis against some of the great tennis players, he probably realized, 'You know what? This guy across the net has as much talent as I do and what is it going to be that separates me from him?' I'm sure when Sidney Green was lining up against some of the great power forwards of the NBA, he probably said, 'You know what? This guy is as good as I am. What am I going to do?' I think that's helped those kids understand that talent is a part of it, but the mental preparation and how hard you and your team play and winning are what it's all about."

Joakim Noah said his father let him learn much about competition on his own.

"We speak about things and he'll give me advice, but he lets me do my own thing," said Joakim. "He was never like, 'You can't do this,' when I was a kid. He never did that." Joakim said he tried tennis when he was a kid, thinking he might want to follow in his father's footsteps, but, "I quit after a couple of days."

Taurean Green's father introduced him to basketball when he was an infant, according to the *Post*. Sidney bought his son a miniature basketball after seeing him flick his right wrist in a shooting motion in the crib. One time, when Sidney played for the Chicago Bulls, he had teammate Michael Jordan touch Taurean's head to bless him as a basketball player.

By the time Taurean became a highly recruited high school guard, his father was coach at Florida Atlantic University. "Having somebody that played the game and coached the game, it helps to hear his opinion on the game of basketball," Taurean said.

Sidney, who played at UNLV and was one game away from going to the Final Four, had one piece of advice for the Gators before they took on UCLA. Recalled Taurean, "He told me to tell my team to just go out and have fun and seize the moment."

"A lot of guys at the big schools might take the tournament for granted. But for the mid-majors and smaller, this is the biggest deal around. This puts us in the same sentence with the elite teams."
—Davidson guard Brendan Winters, before his No. 15 seed team lost in the opening round of the 2006 tourney

DID YOU KNOW . . .

• The back-to-back champion Duke Blue Devils in 1991 and 1992 started two players whose fathers were famous athletes. Grant Hill is the son of Calvin Hill, a star running back in the NFL from 1969 through 1981. Guard Thomas Hill Jr., is the son of Thomas Hill Sr., a world-class hurdler, who earned a bronze medal in the 110-meter event in the 1972 Olympics.

ABOUT
THE AUTHOR

Allan Zullo has penned more than 90 nonfiction books on a wide variety of subjects, including more than two dozen books on sports. He was the co-author of the best-selling 11-book *Sports Hall of Shame* series, which celebrated the wacky and silly side of athletics. Zullo lives with his wife Kathryn near Asheville, North Carolina.

For more information about the author, please go to www.allanzullo.com.

Photography Credits